WHAT CAN I FIND AT THE BEACH?

WALKING THE CAROLINAS BEACHES

GRAZIA WALKER

AUTHOR

Gotham Books

30 N Gould St.
Ste. 20820, Sheridan, WY 82801
https://gothambooksinc.com/

Phone: 1 (307) 464-7800

Published by Gotham Books (date published June 1, 2022)

ISBN: 978-1-956349-72-6 (Paperback)
ISBN: 978-1-956349-73-3 (ebook)

To my grandchildren Camryn, Ian and Sydney
and to my former students around the
world.

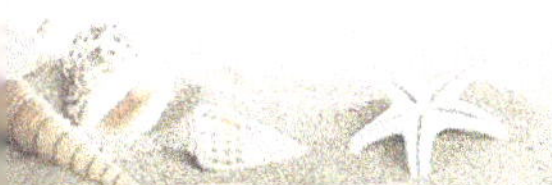

Contents

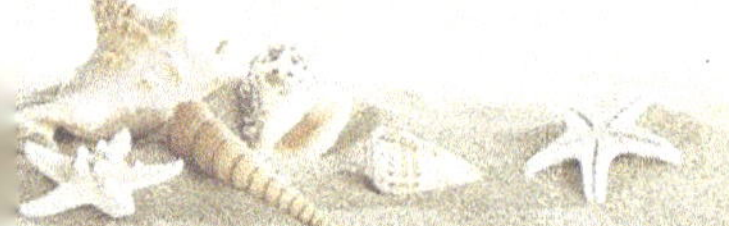

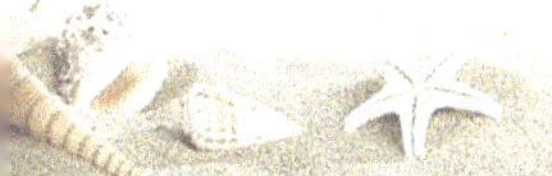

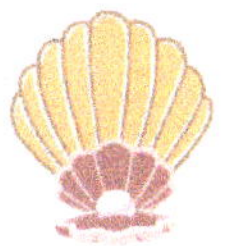

Introduction

The purpose of this book is to foster in adults and children curiosity about the ocean. The beach is where the ocean meets the land and therefore we can learn a lot about the ocean by observing what is left on the beach. This book is for you, a beach walker, who wonders about how shells are formed and what happened to them along the way. You will be able to find and learn about the delicate and beautiful little shells, fragments of colorful shells polished by the ocean, and other items brought to the beach by waves. You would be able to find the life story of some broken shells: how did they live and how did they die? Did they spend most of their time buried in the mud? Where to go? You will be able to find interesting things on every beach. Specifically, in the Outer Banks you will find a great abundance and variety of shells and mermaid's purses. At Edisto beach, for instance, you may find corals, pen shells, horseshoe crabs, and sponges.

Preparation for Walking on the Beach

Consult the tide chart: the best time to go is two hours before low tide and one hour after.

If possible, go to the beach after a storm: the big waves bring in lots of debris.

Go through the debris thoroughly looking for big and small things.

I suggest you walk the same beach twice, one time close to the water and the other time high on the beach.

You should have protection for your feet: sandals would be fine.

Sunscreen is a must, even if the sky is cloudy

Also you'll need:
Thin multipurpose gloves
A magnifying glass
A Backpack so your hands are free
Two plastic bags: one for the things you want to collect and one for garbage.

What do I see?
Sand, lots of sand
Origin

The Outer Banks of North Carolina and the islands along the coast of South Carolina are piles of sand. Most of the sand comes from land and was brought to the sea by rivers over the period of millions of years when the ocean level was lower due to thick polar ice caps. The Appalachian Mountains used to be very high; rain and rivers moved the material to the plain, and then to the ocean. The sand accumulated at the side of the estuary, where the river met the ocean. When the ocean level slowly rose because of the melting of the polar ice caps, little by little the water covered part of the land, the piles of sand became islands and the covered land became a marsh or a shallow water lagoon. The rivers are still bringing water and sand to lagoons and marshes. Tidal inlets, big or small channels, connect lagoons and marshes to the ocean. Some sand comes also from the ocean. Small waves push ashore sand and shells from deep water. Big waves instead move the sand from the beach to the water. Long shore currents are parallel to the beach and move sand along the beach. When they encounter an obstacle such as a pier, they deposit the sand. After depositing the sand, long shore currents continue their path along the coast but instead of depositing sand to the beach they take it away. Some patches of sand are brown: some minerals are brown. The color could also come from little fragments of shells, originally white, which changed color. Shells contain proteins and within the proteins are molecules of iron. The iron combines with the oxygen in the air to form limonite, which is light brown. The process is very slow, so the brown fragments are very old. The islands along the coast of North Carolina and South Carolina are usually connected to land by causeways or bridges. Between the islands and the land are shallow water lagoons and marshes. Marshes are called the nursery of the sea because several fish and invertebrates lay their eggs there. The vegetation, mostly sea grasses, offers a safe place for the eggs to hatch and gives protection to the little fish. The marshes are also rich in nutrients that, on high tide, are exported to the open ocean. Turtles make their egg nests at South Carolina and Georgia beaches. During the nesting period the people living in houses along the beaches are asked to turn off the lights toward the beach in order avoid confusing the mother turtles. The female turtles come at night to the beach they were born. They make a hole in the sand and lay the eggs in such a way that approximately half of the eggs hatch as male, and half hatch as female. The sex of the turtles depends on the temperature of the sand around the egg, not on X and Y-chromosomes as in humans. It is amazing how the mother turtle could arrange the eggs in the sand in such a way that the eggs hatch at different temperatures. Every morning volunteers from the local Marine Research Center check the beach for turtle tracks, find the location of the nest and block it offwith red tape. The visitors should respect the areas blocked by the tape, as to avoid any accidents that might compromise the young turtles' safety.

Composition

The sand contains mineral grains coming from the breaking down of the rocks present on land. Every mineral present on land sooner or later ends up at the beach. Fragments of precious stones are present in the sand but in small amounts undetectable by the naked eye. Since granite is one of the main components of North Carolina and South Carolina rocks, and since quartz is the main mineral in granite, quartz is the main component of the sand there. Quartz is a very hard mineral, and is transparent. Under a magnifying glass the sand appears to be made mostly of little pieces of glass; the black specks are minerals containing iron. The Carolinas sand contains few little pieces of shells. On tropical islands far from land, the sand is mainly made of fragments of shells and of foraminifera, one-cell animals.

Sand from the Outer Bank seen under a microscope. X20

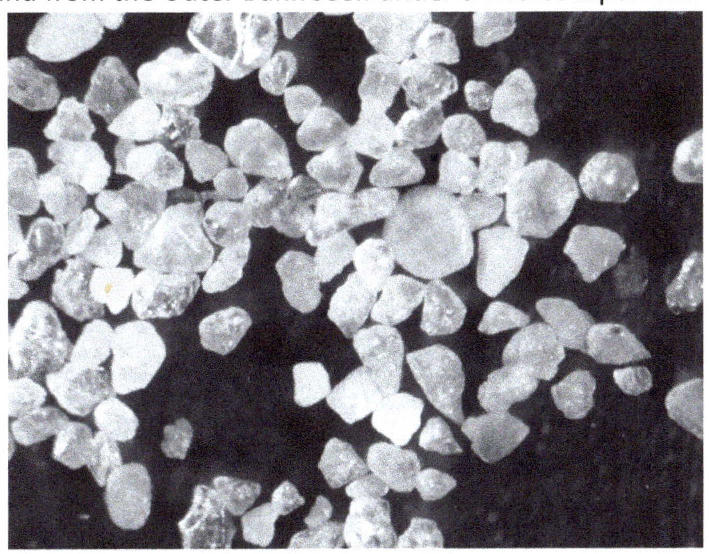

The sand is home of very small and very diverse small animals that cannot be seen by the naked eye. They are less than half of a millimeter long, and they are small enough that they can crawl between the grains of sand without moving them. They feed on bacteria, detritus -particles of dead organic matter- and each other. They are protozoans-one cell animals-, worms, copepods, rotifers, and many others.

Strand Line (Wrack Line)

Strand line is where the majority of the debris is left by the waves at high tide. Some high tides are higher than others; therefore there is often more than one strand line.
Each strand line is parallel to the ocean and often has mounds of wood sticks. The sticks come mostly from the vegetation present in the marshes located between the island and the

land. The high tide takes water to the marshes, collects nutrients and loose vegetation and takes everything to the ocean side via the inlets. Eventually the vegetation ends up to the beach. A good place to find shells is under the wood sticks.

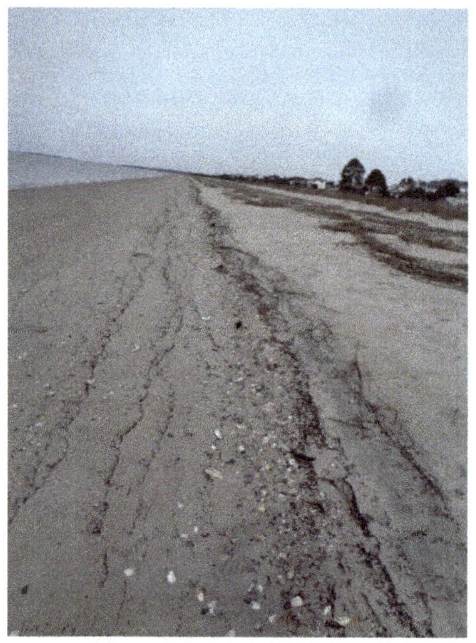

Strand Line

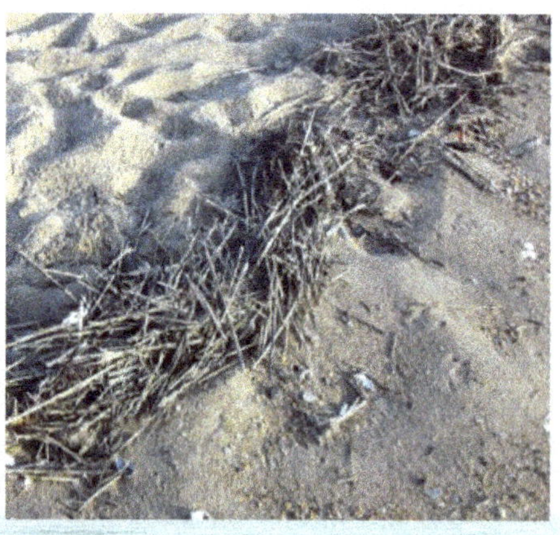

Wood sticks along the strand line

If you see living creatures such as living shells or sea cucumbers in the intertidal area, very gently put them back in the water. Before placing things in your bag examine them carefully, one by one. It is a rock? Is it a part of an animal? A plant? Any pattern? Color? Does it have holes? Plants do not have holes, animals have holes: a mouth to eat food. Ifit is a snail shaped shell, check if it has a hermit crab inside. Breath into the shell and the hermit crab will stick out its head. In this case, the shell should be placed back into the sand. Take as many shells as you want but do not put them in the garbage, Shells are made of Calcium Carbonate. little by little, the water removes the calcium Carbonate. Living mollusks take the calcium carbonate dissolved in the water to make or enlarge the shell.
Look and enjoy the delicate little shells, and the colorful shell pieces. All of them have a story to tell you.

White and Dark Sand

The white sand comes mostly by the breaking down of rocks brought down to the ocean by rivers. With your hand lenses you can see the transparent white grains of quartz. In the upper intertidal zone are patches of polished shell pieces and small pieces of sea glass. Sand and waves grind down and polish the pieces of shells until the edges become smooth, but color and patterns are maintained. Sea glasses are pieces of bottles, glass balls, or other glass material that ended up in the ocean and are ground down. Often closer to the water are very thin patches of grey/black sand. Large waves at high tide remove the top layer of the beach, the white sand, and expose the darker layer containing iron and titanium oxides, the heaviest component of sand.

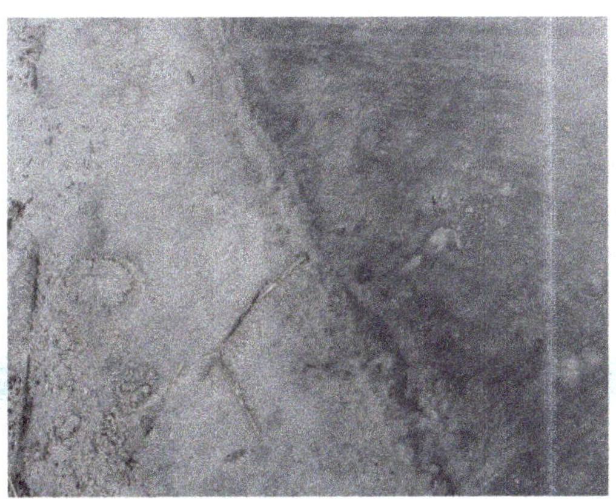

Thick layers of black sand are found deeper in the sand. They contain bacteria processing organic material without oxygen. Recycling of organic materials occurs in every environment and is done by bacteria and fungi. When we talk about organic material- detritus- we talk about dead plants and animals, feces of animals, and food left by people at the beach. When a dead fish is brought by waves the to shore it is first attacked by birds, then crabs, small organisms living within the sand feed on the juice, and finally bacteria take over. After all the energy within the organic material is taken out, what is left is carbon dioxide and mineral. In the white sand the process of decomposition is carried out by bacteria that use the oxygen present in the water circulating between the grains of sand. Deep in the sand, where water does not circulate, there is no oxygen. In that environment the decay bacteria that do not need oxygen carry out process. These anaerobic bacteria produce hydrogen sulfide, which combines with iron to form iron sulfide, a black compound. Black shells are common and noticeable on white sand. Originally they were white then ended up in the oxygen-poor environment, usually mud; in the mud the hydrogen sulfide combined with the iron present in their shell. Eventually wave action brought the shells up to the surface. Their black color stands up on the white sand. The grey shells spent less time in the black layer. Different shells need different amounts of time to change color.

Along the beach, close to the water, after a storm you could see foam. It is not soap foam; it is POM, Particulate Organic Matter. The strong waves stir up the bottom sediments, releasing the organic matter, mostly protein and diatoms, present there. The ocean water is like a broth, containing organic matter in solution, DOM, Dissolved Organic Matter. The difference between DOM and POM is the amount of organic matter present in the water: small quantity of organic matter, DOM, large quantity of organic matter, POM. DOM is not visible with the naked eye, POM looks like soap foam. The diatoms are one-cell algae with a shell made of glass. They are the ones that make the rocks in the intertidal area very slippery.

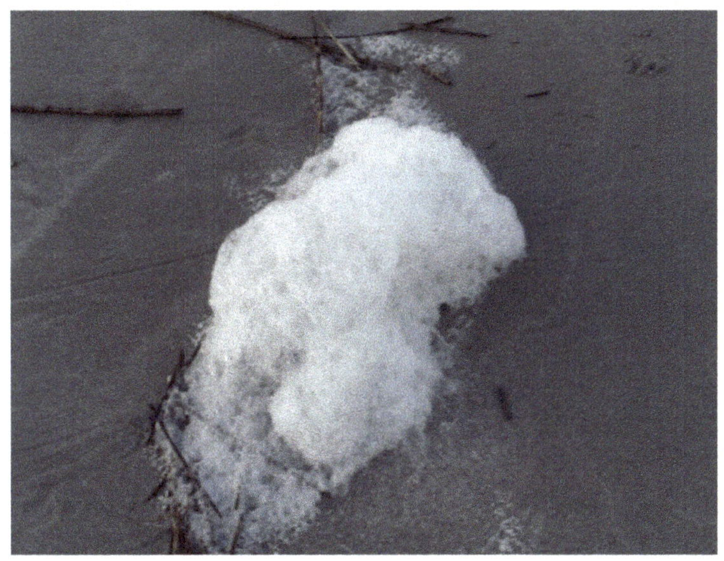

POM

Big and Small Holes in the Sand

The big holes on the beach are burrows of ghost crabs. Notice that they are slanted, leaning toward the water. Inside there could be several chambers and often a connection with another hole. The nest could reach a depth offour feet. During low tide there are several birds in the intertidal area, all looking for food. Crabs are very appetizing to birds. Beside protection during low tide, the nests could be used during the molting period. Crabs have an outside skeleton therefore when they get bigger they have to shed the skeleton and make a new one. The newly molted crab is soft and vulnerable so it hides until the hardening of the new skeleton. Soft-shell crabs are crabs that have just molted. Usually fishermen take adult blue crabs from the ocean, keep them in a tank and feed them well until they molt. In low-energy beaches, where the waves are small, it is very easy to find empty crab shells that are intact. To see if it is a dead crab or an empty shell without picking it up, look at the eyes. If they are transparent, it is a shell. The gills are left in the old shells because they are clogged with fine sediments.

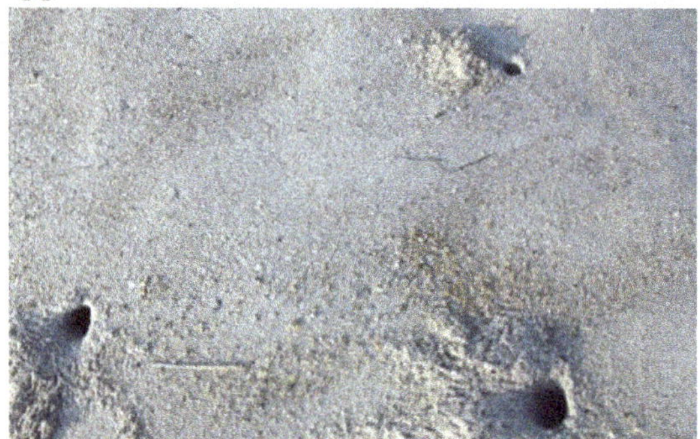

Burrows of ghost crabs

Mole crab or sand crab lives in the zone of breaking waves. It borrows backward into the sand, facing incoming waves. With its feathery antennas it collects food from the backwash of each wave.

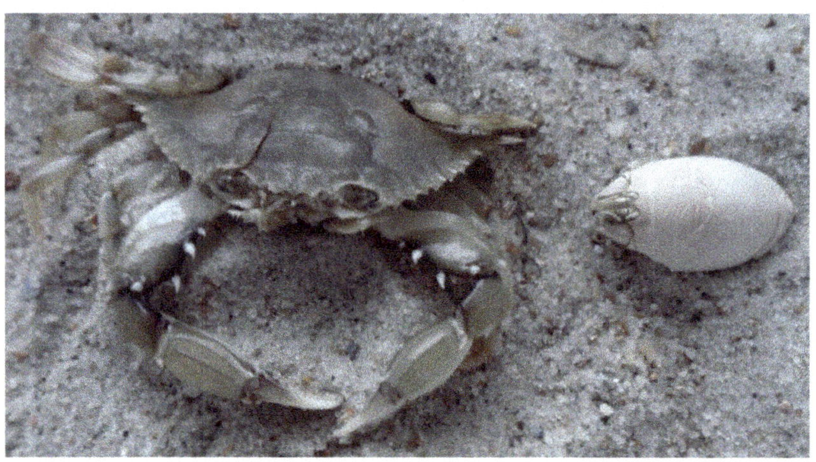

Ghost crab and mole crab empty shells

Small holes in the intertidal area are due to a physical process. Strong waves during high tide push air and water into the sand. During low tide air and water find their way out from the sand through small holes.

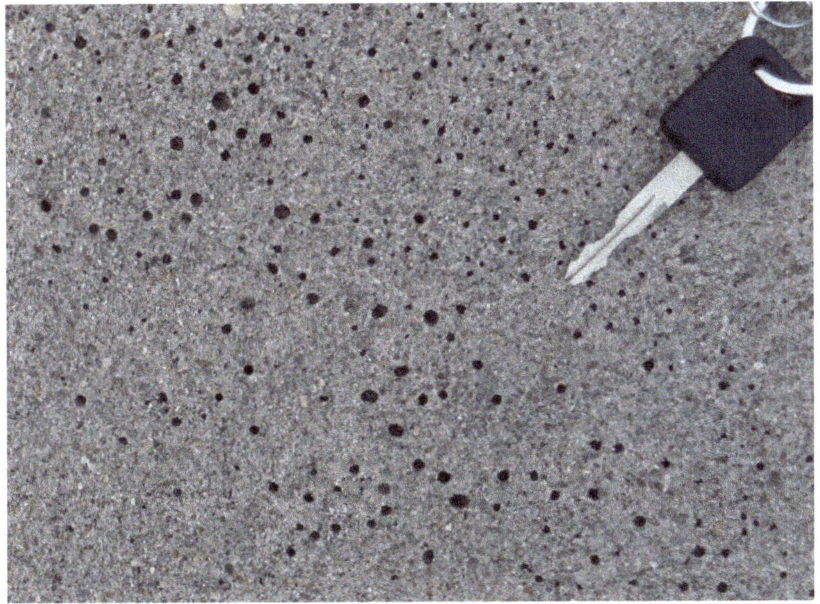

Small holes in the intertidal area

Ways animals adapt to
life in the ocean

Ocean environment is very different from land environment; therefore the animals develop different survival strategies. Animals living on land are surrounded by air, which does not contain food, and therefore they spend much energy searching for food. The ocean is a broth of organic materials: animals can attach to a substrate and filter the water passing by getting all the nutrients they need without spending much energy. Many marine animals are filter feeders; the size of the particle they can ingest varies greatly. Sponges absorb only small organic particles dissolved in the water, corals bring in copepods and other small plankton, baleen whale bring in small fish. On land the closest animal to use the filter feeding mechanism is the spider: it filters the air with its web. Most of the filter feeders are attached to a substrate: a stone, a shell, or a baby sock.

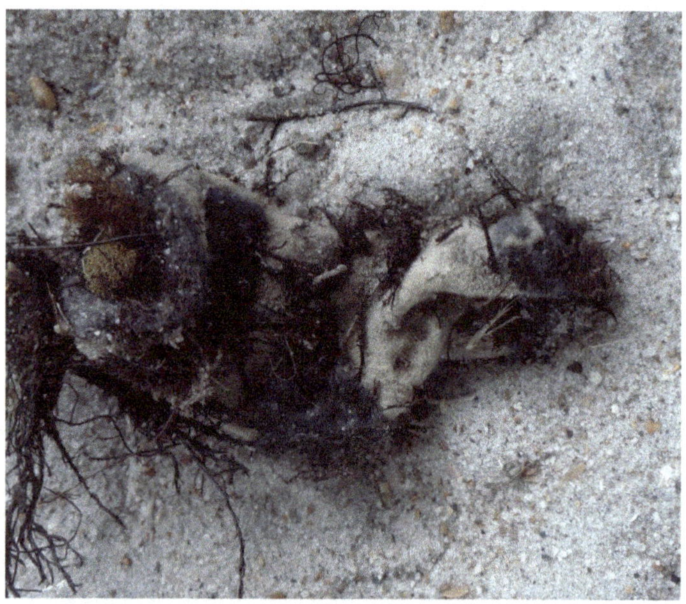

Baby sock, home of sponges, seaweeds,
sticks, and many small animals

Marine animals spend less energy than land ones moving from one place to another because of the buoyancy of water. Except for some areas around the coast, marine animals have no physical protection from predators; the ocean is an open space, no rocks, and no leaves where they can hide. Therefore, they develop ways to protect themselves from predators: the cone shells developed venomous darts; sponges make stinky and foul tasting chemicals. Fish living on top of the water are blue on the dorsal side and white on the ventral side; the birds cannot distinguish the blue of the fish from the blue of the water and the big fish below see the white that blends with the sky. Reproduction in marine animals is different than in land animals. On land the reproduction is by internal fertilization; in the ocean most of the time fertilization of the eggs occurs in the water and the larvae spend time as plankton completely independent from their parents. Respiration is also different. Animals living in water take in the oxygen dissolved in the water. Oxygen is not a limiting factor for land animals but it is for animals living in the water because the amount of oxygen in the solution is a function of water temperature: the warmer the water, the less oxygen in the solution. The oxygen dissolved in the water is taken in at the gills. Gills have the same function as our lungs; they both are the sites of gas exchange: oxygen is taken in and carbon dioxide is moved out. Animals that have gills need to be in the water to breath. Marine mammals and reptiles possess lungs and they take the oxygen from the air. If mammals live in the water, they need to come up to breath. Sea snakes have lungs extending from the stomach almost to the tail allowing them to stay in the water for up to 1 0 hours. Most of the marine animals are carnivorous: they eat any animal smaller than themselves. They have developed adaptations to protect them from being eaten and for catching food. Often the same structure serves as a protection and a way to catch a prey. Stinging cells protect jellyfish but also catch a meal. The water temperature does not fluctuate as much as the temperature on land and many marine organisms are adapted to live in a narrow temperature range. The corals that form coral reefs grow in water at temperature around 68-degrees F.

At higher temperatures, the corals expel the zooxantellae algae, their source of sugar and oxygen, and appear white; they look like have been bleached with Clorox. They do not stay white for long: algae, seaweeds, soft corals, and other encrusting organisms attach to the bare coral skeleton.

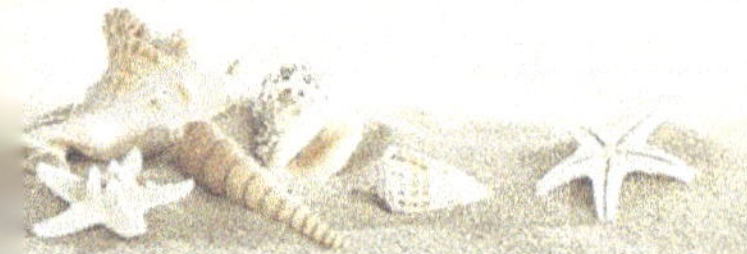

Common Findings at the beach

Shells; Lots of Shells

The findings are not the same at every beach because waves and long-shore currents affect what is deposited on the beach. Big waves can carry to the beach big shells, small waves small shells. Long-shore currents parallel to the beach can move shells from one place to another in the water along the beach. In addition, organisms living in the water could be different from place to place. Mermaid's purses are very abundant at Nags Head on the Outer banks of North Carolina. Going south, still at the Outer Banks, the number of Mermaid's purses decreases until they are very rare. Since Mermaid's purses are egg cases of skates, it means that more skates live in the northern part ofthe coast. At Edisto beach in South Carolina, on one side of a small pier I found only shells. On the other side, beside shells, I found empty shell of horseshoe crabs and several branches of black gorgonian coral. Therefore, you will not be able to see on one beach everything mentioned in this book. Explore the beach, look at the little things, recognize the wonderful work of nature, and have fun!

What is a shell? How is the shell made?

The shell is the shield the animal builds around itself for protection. The animal belongs to the large group of mollusks, soft-body animals. The mantle, the very thin membrane entirely covering the living animal, makes the shell. Directions for making its shape and its outside pattern are in the DNA of the mantle cells. The material needed to make the shell comes from the food eaten by the animal. The process is similar to building a house: the mantle first makes a protein frame, and then fills it with bricks of calcium carbonate taken from the water. The color comes from pigments present in the food the animal eats; therefore some species could have the same basic shape and pattern but slightly different colors depending on the food available in that area. In the main part of the shell, to make it strong, the bricks are placed perpendicular to its surface. The inside, to make the surface smooth, has the bricks in layers parallel to the surface. As the animal grows, the shell grows, just like the skeleton of a child grows over the years. Just like when we break a bone we can repair it, the mollusks can repair their shell by adding bricks from the inside. The animal looses the shell only after death; it never changes its shell. It cannot live without its shell. The shell is different from a skeleton because it does not have living cells, only the mantle has living cells. Our skeleton has living cells, blood, and nerves. It is renewing itself constantly, cell by cell. It is calculated that approximately every seven years we have a new skeleton. The shell does not possess living cells and blood, but it can get bigger: the mantle adds new calcium carbonate bricks on the outside margin. In gastropods the mantle cells not only are able to add bricks, but can also take away bricks from one place and adding them to another. Hermit crabs, first cousins of lobster, are born with a tender tail and they use an empty shell as their home to protect their tail. When they outgrow the shell they have to find another one. It is interesting to see a hermit crab looking for a bigger shell: it tries different ones and when it finds the perfect one, it brushes out any grain of sand lodged in the shell with the little broom at the end of its tail. Grains of sand would damage its delicate tail.

Bleached and Black Shells

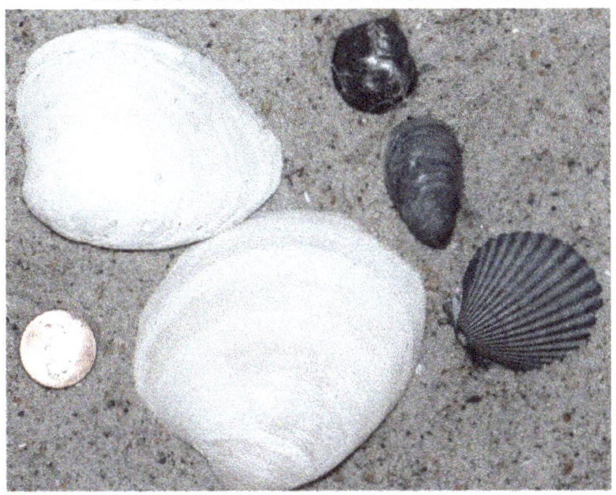

The sun makes shells loose their shine and gradually makes them chalky white, giving the appearance of being bleached. The black shells spent time in an oxygen-poor mud present in the lagoon, the area between islands and land. There, bacteria break down organic material and release hydrogen sulfide, the rotten eggs smelling gas. Hydrogen sulfide reacts with the iron present in the shell forming iron sulfide, a black compound. The more time the shell spends in the mud, the darker it becomes. Some shells, such as the thin jingle shell, blacken very quickly, whereas the thicker ones require more time. All black shells are old and some are very old, 10,000 to 1.8 million years old.

What do mollusks eat?

Some mollusks are herbivores, feeding on algae, some are carnivores, feeding on dead or alive animals, and others are filter feeders, trapping small organic material from the water.

How do Mollusks breathe?

Just like all the invertebrates living in the ocean, the mollusks take in the oxygen dissolved in the water. The water molecule contains oxygen, but only plants can break the strong bond between oxygen and hydrogen and release the oxygen.

The oxygen dissolved in water is taken in through the gills, by a process called diffusion. Just like in our lungs, the membrane in the filaments is very thin and allows gas molecules to go through. Since there is more oxygen in the outside water, more oxygen molecules will enter the filament than exit. The opposite is for carbon dioxide: more molecules will exit rather than enter. The water temperature affects the amount of oxygen dissolved in the water: the higher the temperature, the less oxygen is retained. You can easily prove this point by placing a pot of tap water on a burner. Long before reaching the boiling point, small bubbles appear at the bottom ofthe pan; they are air bubbles kicked out by the water molecules that, because of the higher temperature, moved faster.

How do Mollusks reproduce?

All of them reproduce sexually. Some mollusks are only female or only male; others are both male and female in the same animal. Fertilization of the egg can occur inside the female body or outside, in the water. In some mollusks the female lays the fertilized eggs in gelatinous masses, in capsule, or in strings. The capsule could contain one egg or more, sometimes close to 1,000 eggs. The fertilized egg develops into a larva (the youngest stage, after hatching from the egg), which is carried around by waves and currents. Most of the larvae end up as food of hungry animals. When the survived larva settles down, the mantle starts developing the first shell. This new shell is very thin; therefore it is seldom present in the adult. In some gastropods the tip of the adult shell has different color from the rest of the shell: it is the first shell.

How do Mollusks move?

The gastropods, the snail looking mollusks, possess a strong foot and most of them crawl. Most bivalves, the clam looking mollusks,

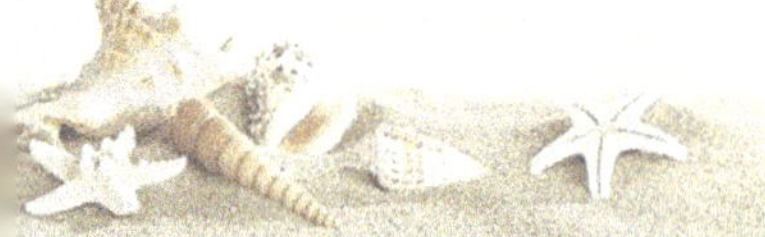

possess a foot designed to dig in the sand. Some, like the jackknives, burrow rapidly into sand. Other bivalves, such as mussels and oysters, do not move.

Do Mollusks have eyes?

Gastropods, snail looking ones, do have eyes but in some of them the eyes can only detect light intensity. Bivalves, the clam looking ones, have ocelli, primitive eyes that can detect sudden changes in light intensity. Mollusks do not see very well but they can smell and taste the water.

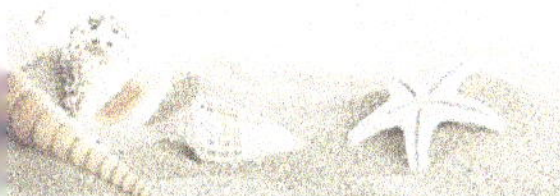

Two Main Kinds of Shells:

Gastropods and Bivalves

Gastropods: Snail Looking Shells

General Characteristics

Gastro means stomach, pod means foot. Gastropod: crawling on the stomach. The shell is made of only one piece. Most of them have a trap door, the operculum, to close the shell and protect the inside animal from predators. The operculum could be thick and heavy like the one in turban shells, or very thin and made of protein like in periwinkles. It is attached to the posterior dorsal part of the foot. After death the operculum separates from the animal. This large group of mollusks includes periwinkles, conchs, slipper snails, moon snail, cowries, and murexes. Most of them possess a radula: small circular teeth on a circular ribbon functioning as a scraper. Most of them are carnivorous and some of them such as the moon shell and the murexes, dig holes into a living shell and suck it up alive. The holes made by the moon shell are very well defined, circular. The process of making the hole could take almost a day. The moon shell softens the prey's shell with stomach acid and then scrapes away the limestone with its radular teeth. The predator snail needs to decide where to drill the hole: in a clam, the part close to the margin is the thinnest one but there is the danger that the clam would open and close the valves crushing the predator. A few gastropods, such as the limpets, use their radular teeth to scrape algae from rocks. Other gastropods feed on dead organisms. The knobbed whelk feeds on large bivalves such as oysters using the sharp aperture lip to pry open the shell of the prey. Some cone shells eat live fish: they have radular teeth made into harpoons and they make powerful venom. They shoot the harpoon coated with venom to a fish passing by. The fish is paralyzed and eaten whole on the spot. The venom is so powerful that it can kill a man if the harpoon lands close to his heart. Gastropods reproduce always sexually and they have internal fertilization. Often the fertilized eggs are inside an egg case. Some are only male or female; others are both male and female, however they never have self-fertilization.

Outside and Inside of a Gastropod

Below is the photo of a knobbed whelk. On the right is the animal that built the shell, on the left is the shell itself. In the animal notice how the tail is curled; it is curled because it is wrapped around the columella. The black oval structure on top is the operculum, the trap door designed to protect the animal from intruders.

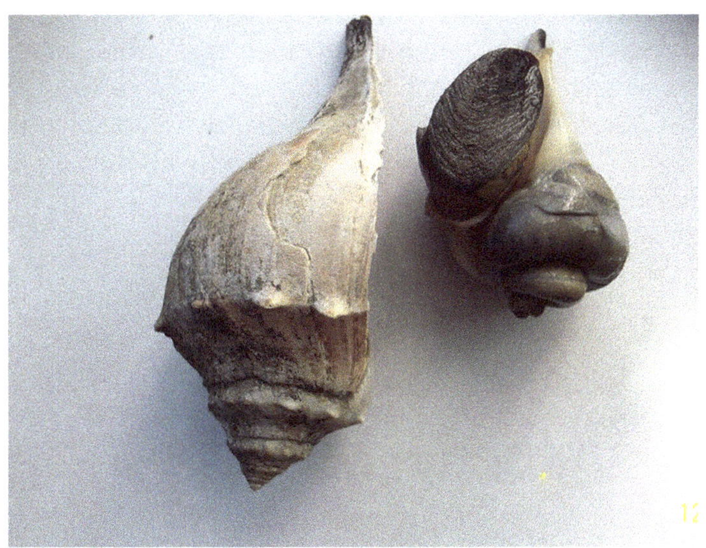

Welk shell

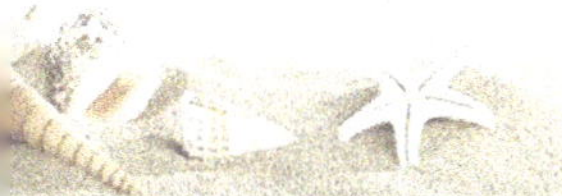

19

Most Common Gastropods and Identifying Features

Moon snails, also called Shark eyes

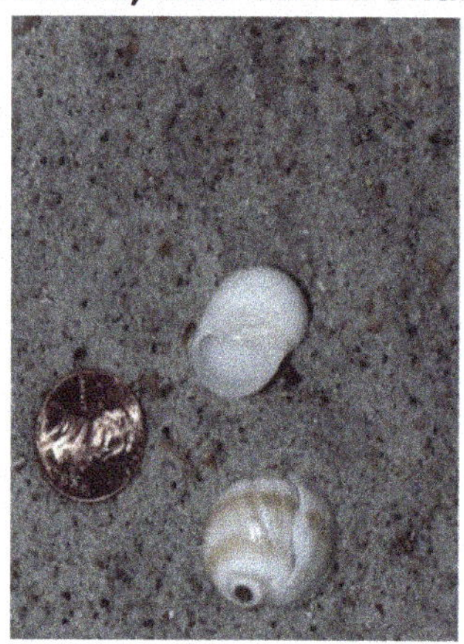

Identifying Features: They have a large opening and a conspicuous "eye" at the tip. They live in the sand and prey upon other shells: they drill holes on shells of living gastropods or bivalves and suck them up alive (See holes in shells). Collar sands on the beach contain moon shell eggs within a mixture of mucus and sand. On the bottom shell, notice a line parallel to the aperture: the shell was cracked when alive and the mantle mended it. The interior, in contact with the soft body, is smooth but the outside has a scar.

Purple snail

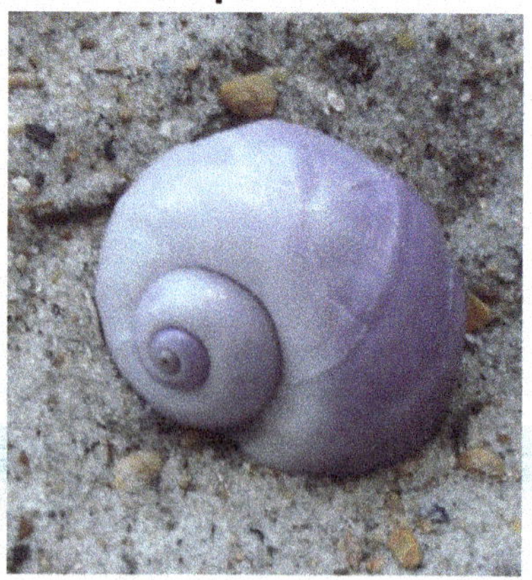

Identifying Features: Purple snails are purple and very thin. These features make the purple snail very well adapted to living on top of the water. To increase buoyancy, they build, with mucus and gas, a small raft in front of the aperture. The raft is like a miniature bubble wrap. Under the raft female purple snails deposit their eggs. Purple snails travel in big groups carried by currents and waves; sometimes they end up on the beach. Stepping on their rafts is like stepping on bubble wrap, the same popping sound.

Worm shell

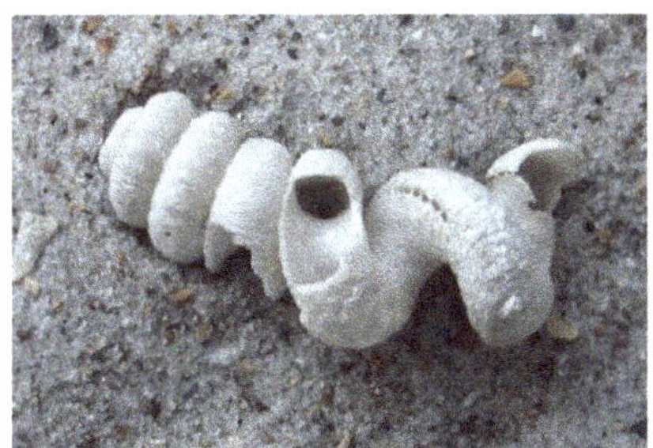

Identifying Features: They have a worm shape. The inside is smooth and shiny (mother-of-pearl layer) since they are mollusks. Worms do not posses a mantle and therefore the inside is rough. They live attached to rocks, other shells, or wooden structure, singly or in large masses. Its white color probably comes from being bleached by the sun.

Slipper snails

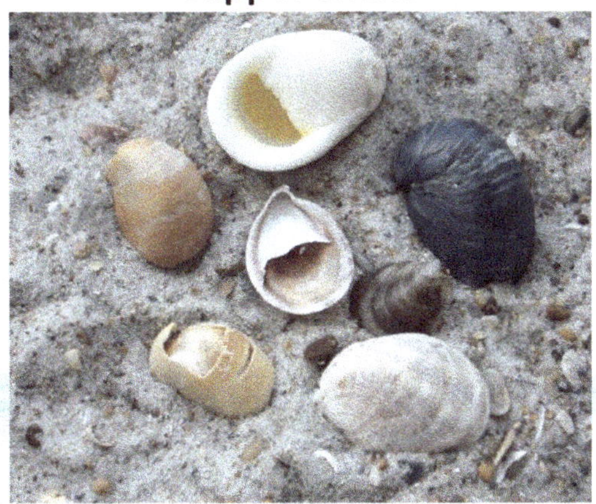

Identifying Features: Their ventral side (where the opening is) has a small shelf. Slipper snails do not like to be alone; they like to live on top of other slipper shells or inside empty shells. They are filter feeders. They can change sex: the young one starts as a male and then changes into a female. The black shell spent time in the anaerobic environment.

White baby ears

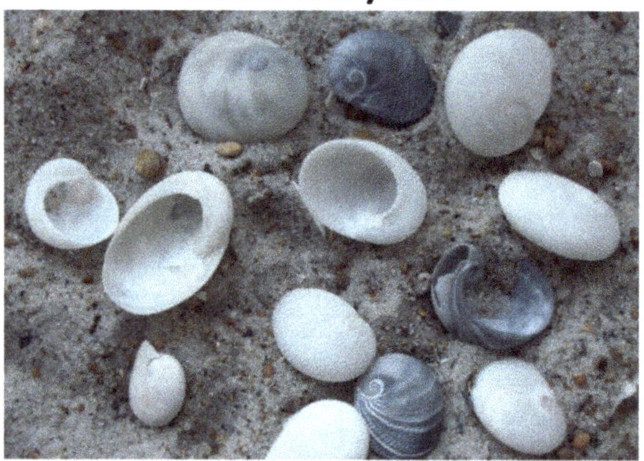

Identifying Feature: Their shells are flat, with a large aperture, the apex slightly turned, and spiral grooves. Since their shells cannot contain the whole body, for protection they slide under the sand. They prey on bivalves. The grey and black ones spent time in an anaerobic environment where the process of decomposition occurs without oxygen. The grey spent less time in that environment than the black one.

Scotch Bonnets shell

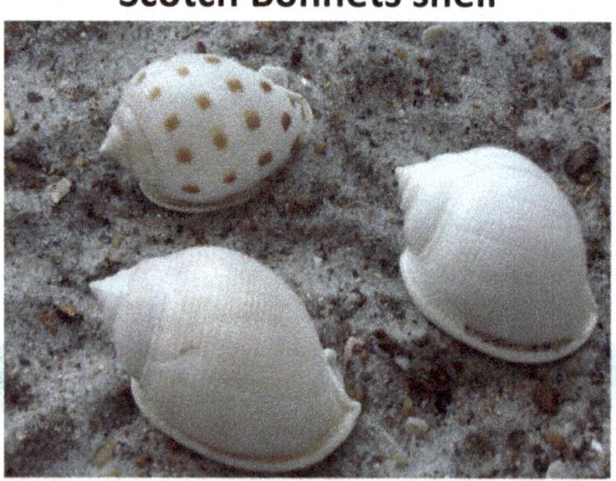

Identifying Features: The Scotch bonnets have a very large aperture. Their outer lip is thick and bears teeth. They have many thin lines parallel to the apex. They have a beautiful shape and pattern. Scotch bonnet is the North Carolina State shell and its name is in honor of its Scot forebears. They live on sand in shallow water. They feed on sand dollars and sea urchins.

Ceritium snails

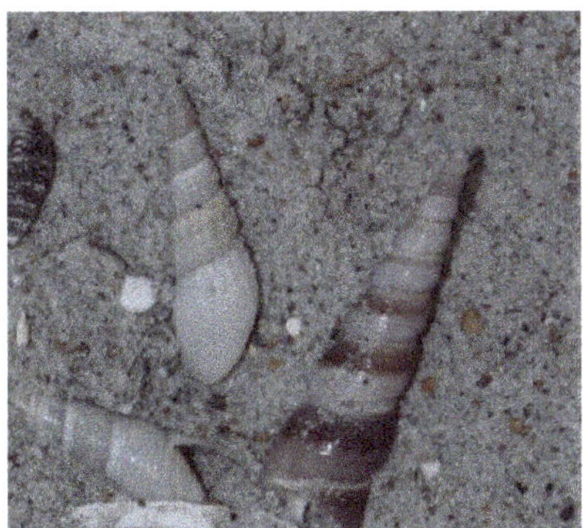

Identifying Features: Ceritiums have a slender shell with a pointed spire.

Their size varies from .3 to 16 cm. The many whorls are variously sculptured.

Most of them live in sandy areas and in rubble mixed with sand. They feed on algae and detritus

Olive snails

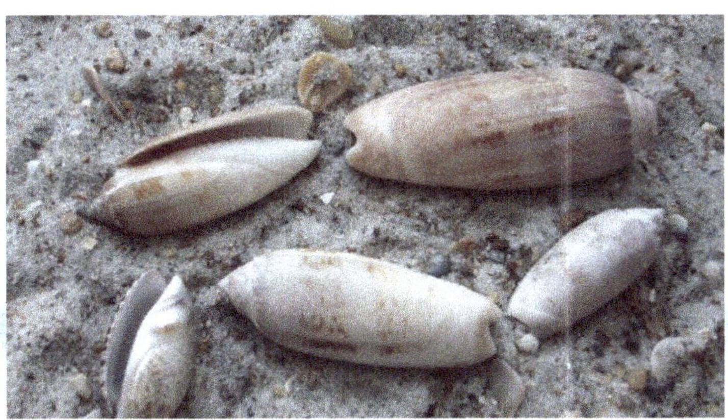

Identifying Features: They possess a thick and very glossy shell, long aperture, and variable markings. The olives live in the sand. Their mantle, not only covers the animal, but also covers the entire shell keeping it shiny. Most of them are scavengers; the lettered olive (left bottom in the figure) preys on clams. The lettered olive is the South Carolina state shell.

Egg cases

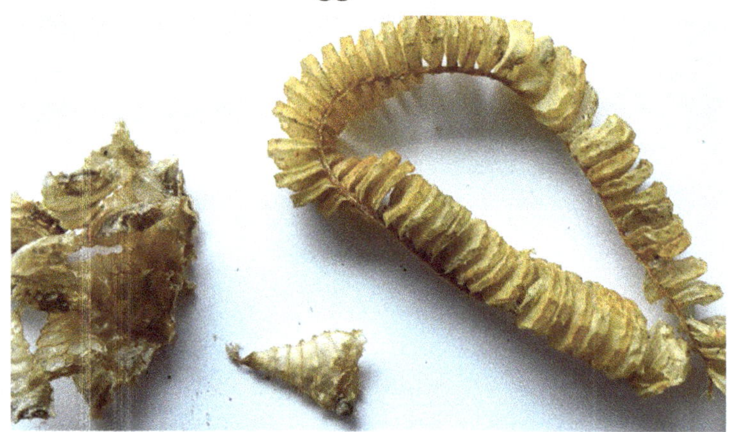

Egg Cases

Several gastropods, snail-like mollusks, lay their eggs in egg cases, usually a long string of small pouches. Each pouch can contain one or more eggs. The eggs develop inside the pouches and then the baby snails move out into the world. Here are two examples of large egg cases commonly found on the beach. The mother gastropod lays the eggs in the water and some end up on the beach. On the right is the egg case of the lightning whelk, on the left of a horse conch. When found on the beach, they are dried up and feel plastic. Notice the different shape: the whelk's is a string of capsules, the conch's are cones bunched together as a bouquet of flowers. The cone in the middle has baby shells inside: for some reason the babies did not leave the nest.

Bivalves: clam looking shells

General Characteristics

Bivalves are the most common shells found in sandy beaches. They possess a large foot designed to dig. On rocky shore the predominant mollusks are the gastropods. They are called Bivalves because they have 2 valves, the shell is made of 2 interlocking pieces, right and left valve which are mirror images of each other. This large group of mollusks includes clams, mussels, coquina clams, and oysters. We eat many of them. The jackknife clam is delicious but very difficult to catch because it digs into the sand very fast. Bivalves are filter feeders; they filter the water that passes through the gills keeping the organic material dissolved. Most bivalves dig into the sand with their strong foot. Some, such as oysters and mussels, are attached to a substrate or to other shells. The mantle is attached to the shell by muscle fibers all along its margin. Occasionally, a grain of sand slips between the mantle and the shell making the mantle react and isolate the intruder by surrounding it with few layers of mother of pearl. Commonly this little pearl becomes embedded in the shell. Special oysters inhabiting the warmer Pacific Ocean are able to make natural pearls adding layer after layer of mother of pearl around the intruder. Greater the number of layers, the greater is the luster of the pearl. The cultured pearls are made by inserting little pearls from fresh water clams into the fold of the mantle of one of those Pacific Ocean oysters. The difference between natural and cultured oysters is in the starter: a natural intruder in the natural pearl, an artificial intruder in the cultured ones. Bivalves have 2 siphons, two little pipes: one draws the water inside the animal; the other pushes the water out. The water passing through the gills leaves oxygen and food and then is moved out. The food is moved toward the stomach where it is digested and absorbed. Bivalves have no head, eyes, or radula. Most bivalves release eggs and sperm in the water where fertilization occurs. The fertilized egg develops into a larva and then, if it survives the dangerous environment, into an adult. The first part of the shell to form is the umbo, the tip of the shell. The lines, more or less pronounced, and parallel to the margin of each valve, are the growth line; they can tell the age of the shell to marine biologists specialized in the field of malacology. Malacology is the science that studies the biology of mollusks. By far the most common bivalve shell in the Carolina beaches is the oyster. Some of the oyster shells are polished to the point that now they are very thin and very flat

Outside and Inside Anatomy of a typical bivalve: the Quahog clam

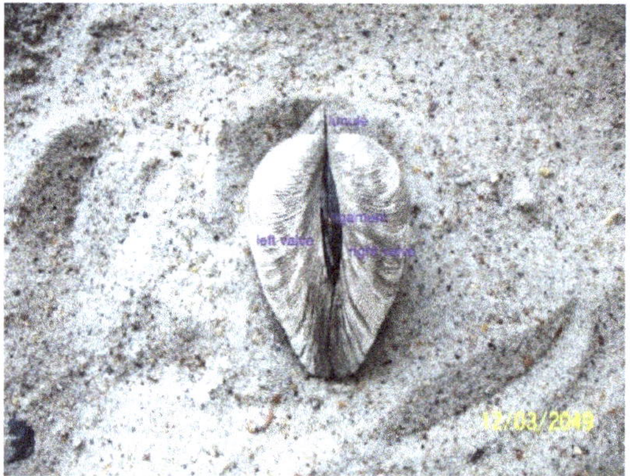

Identifying features:
The shell of the quahog is very thick, its umbone is located near the front end, it has a very distinct lunule, concentric ridges that are strong near the umbone, and three interlocking cardinal teeth atop of each valve.

Ligament: the brown, elastic band that makes the valve open when the muscles relax. Lunule is the oval shape imprint above

the ligament. The lunule is the feature present in every clam. To distinguish right and left valve, place the clam in the above position, with the ligament facing you. The valve on your right is the right valve; the one on your left is the left valve.

Open Quahog Clam showing the 2 valves

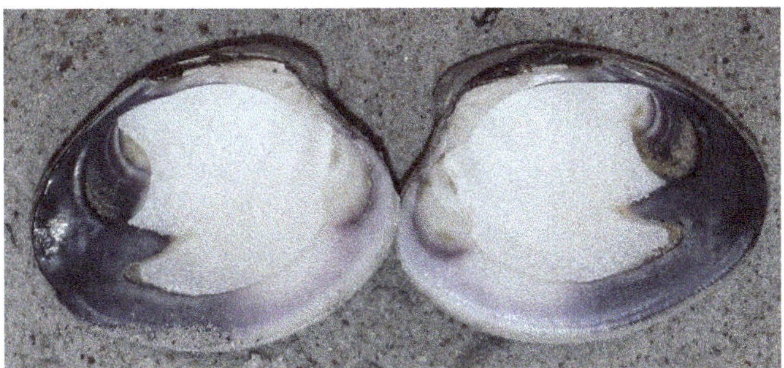

Umbo: an elevated knob, the oldest part ofthe shell.
The pallial line is where the mantle was attached to the shell. Notice the pallial sinus, the place where the 2 siphons in the living animal were located. The mantle is the skin covering the whole animal. The cells in the mantle make the shell. Ifyou find a single valve you can tell ifit is the right or the left valve by checking the position of the pallial sinus, right on the right valve, left on the left valve. The two brown oval spots above each pallial sinus are muscle scars, where the muscles to open the valves where attached.

The Quahog Animal, the soft mollusk inside the shell, the maker of the shell.

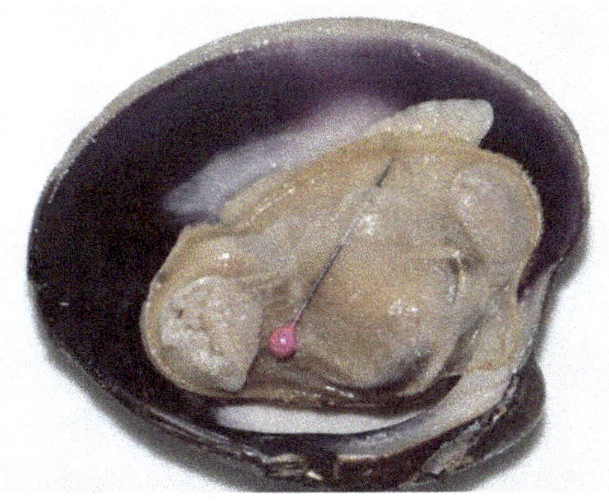

The pin shows the mantle, the thin layer that covers the entire animal. The projections at the margins of the mantle lodge receptors to make the animal aware of the environment. The round mass next to the head ofthe pin is one ofthe 2 muscles- the other one is at the opposite side- that close the valve. The "tongue" sticking out of the mantle is the muscular foot, used to dig into the sand

The mantle was removed to show the part below

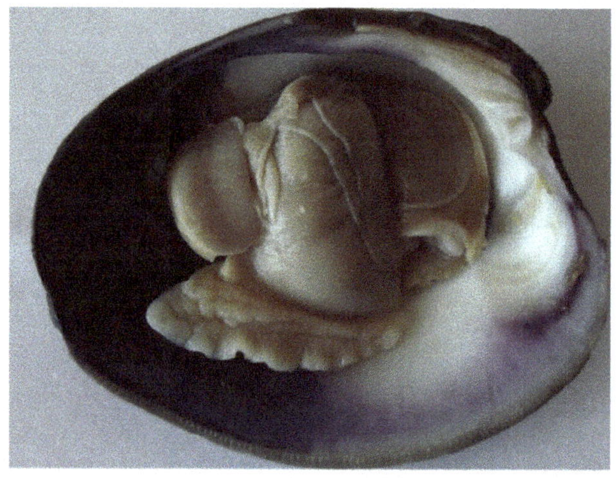

Between the 2 muscles are the 2 gills, made offine filaments. Next to the gills are 2 appendages (palps) and between them is the mouth (hidden). Water passing through the gills leaves oxygen and food. The palps help move the food to the mouth. The thin black line on the right margin, next to the muscle scar, is the exit of the excurrent siphon

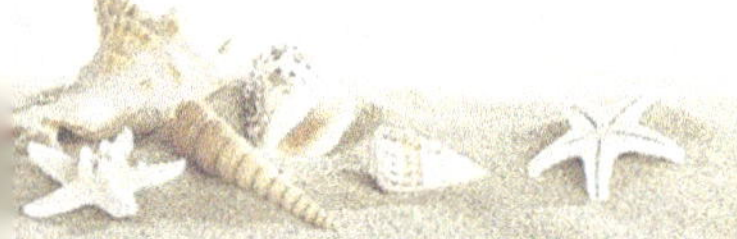

Most Common Bivalves and Identifying Features

Crossed-bar venus clams

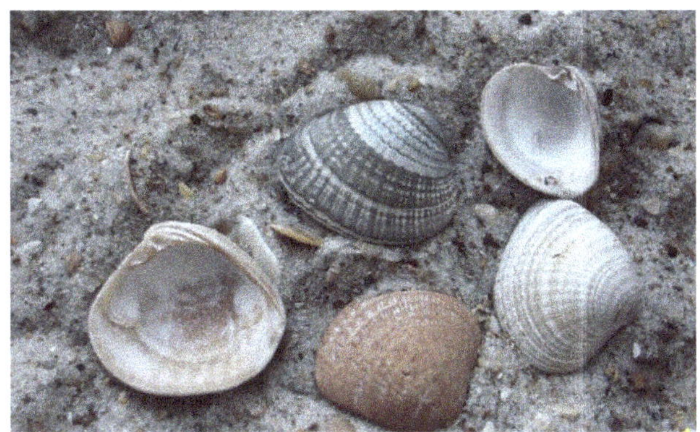

Identifying Features: The shells of these clams are ovate to almost triangular in shape, with a rounded front end. They possess strong concentric ridges and radial ribs. Clams can be grey, light brown, or darker brown in color. Their habitat is sandy bottoms. They are filter feeders.

Surfclams

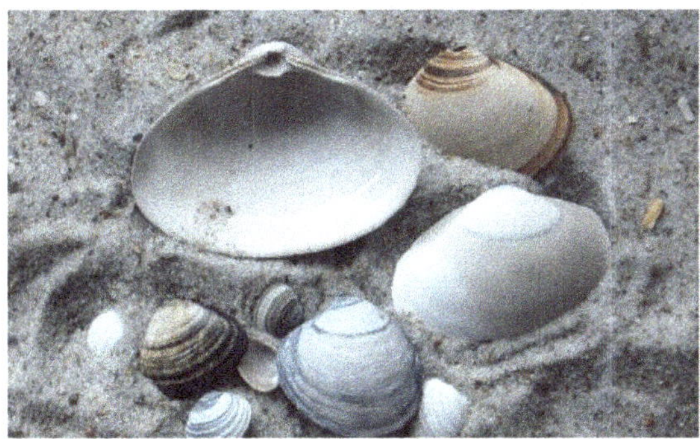

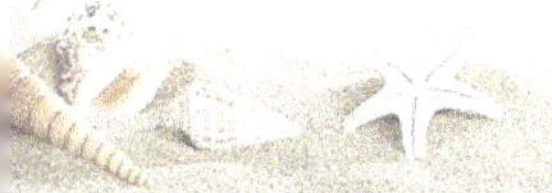

Identifying Features: Surfclams have a spoon-shaped pit behind the hinge teeth. The shells are thin, smooth, and with concentric ridges. Color may be white, cream, and brown, with or without dark growth bands. They are very common at the Outer Banks.

Ark Shells

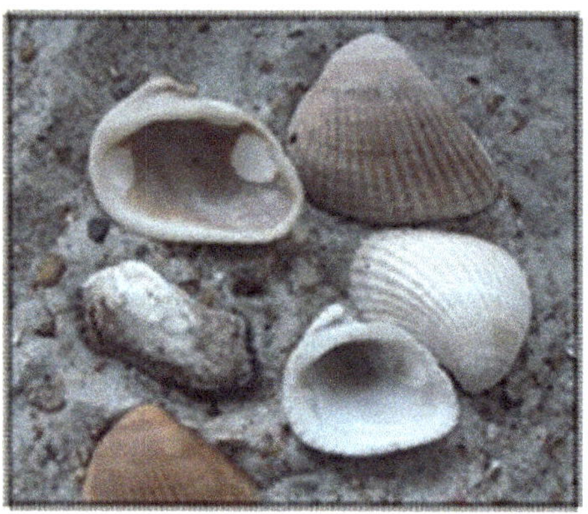

Identifying Features: The shells of arks are thick and elongate. They possess a prominent umbone and a wide hinge line with many teeth. The two oval muscle scars are connected to the pallial line. They possess prominent radial sculpture; some of them have concentric sculpture. They can live in high-energy beaches because their shells are very thick.

Cockles

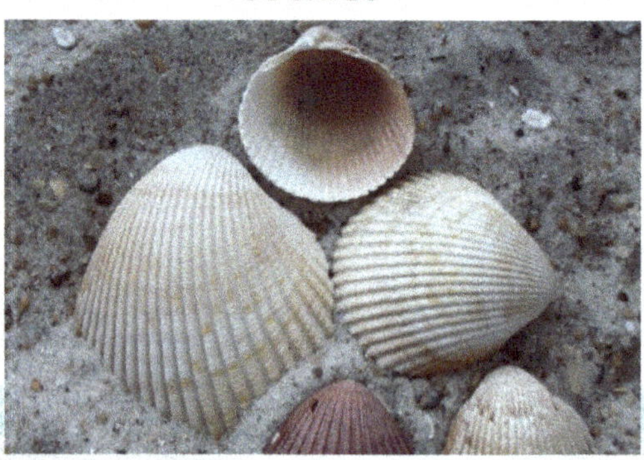

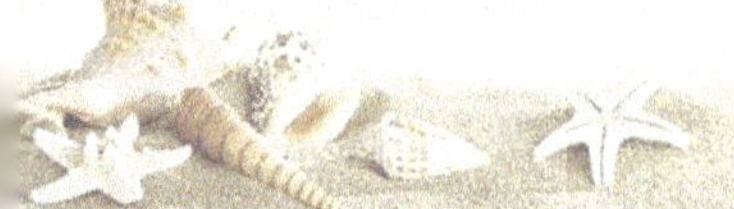

Identifying Features: Cockles are inflated, oval shaped to almost circular. They have prominent radial ribs, frequently spiny, sometime smooth. The umbones are at or near the center of the upper margin. On the inside the external ribbings appear as radial groves. The shell margins are often scalloped. On each valve a central tooth can be found under the umbo. Habitat: sandy bottoms in the intertidal area

Oyster

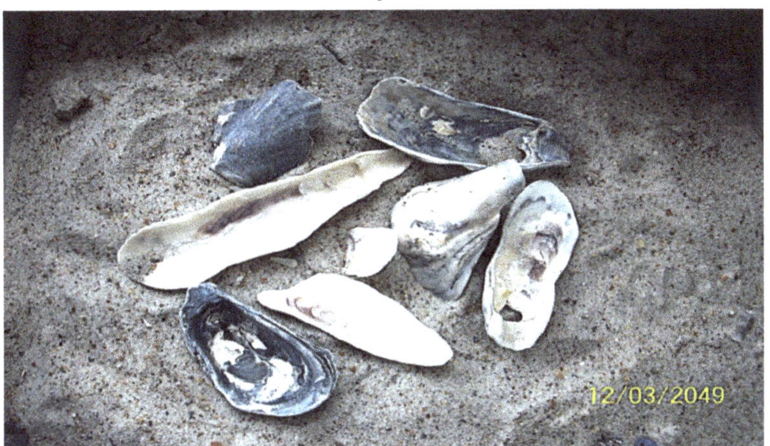

Identifying Features: Oysters are the most common shells in the east coast beaches. They are the common edible oysters. They do not make pearls. Their shell is large, irregular. They live cemented to rocks or other oyster shells. Their right valve is flatter than the left one; it is like a lid over the left, which is attached to the substrate. Oyster harvest has declined in the last few years for several reasons including introduced diseases. Oyster beds are similar to coral reefs in creating habitats for many species of marine life.

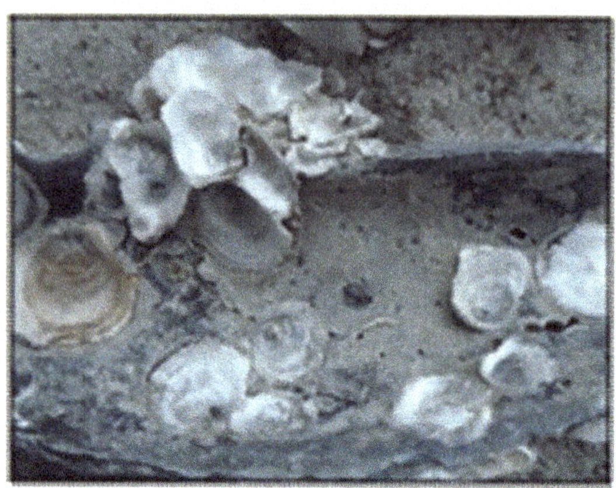

Other oysters and some bryozoans (the 'lace" in the middle) colonized an old oyster shell. Bryozoans are very small but complex animals living in colonies. Each hole in the "lace" was the home of a single bryozoan animal.

Lucine

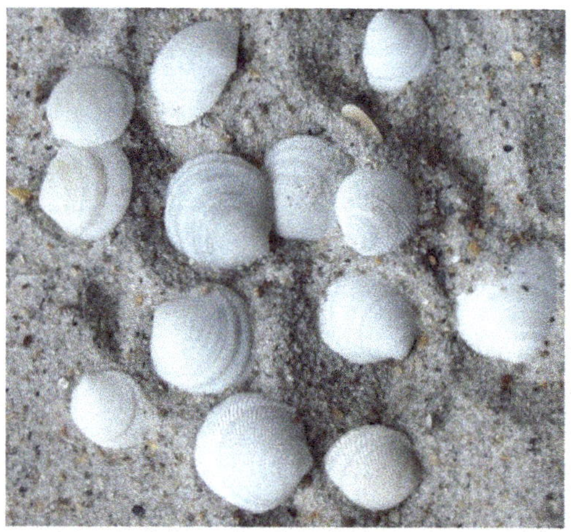

Identifying Features: They are almost circular, have a central umbo, are white; possess diagonal lines and chevron-like grooves. Their interior is white and the margin is very finely toothed. Habitat: sandy, shallow to offshore bottom

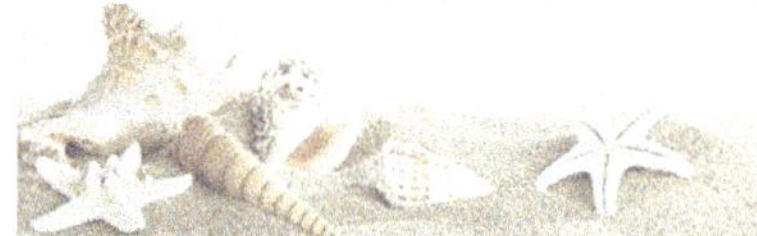

Jacknife Clam

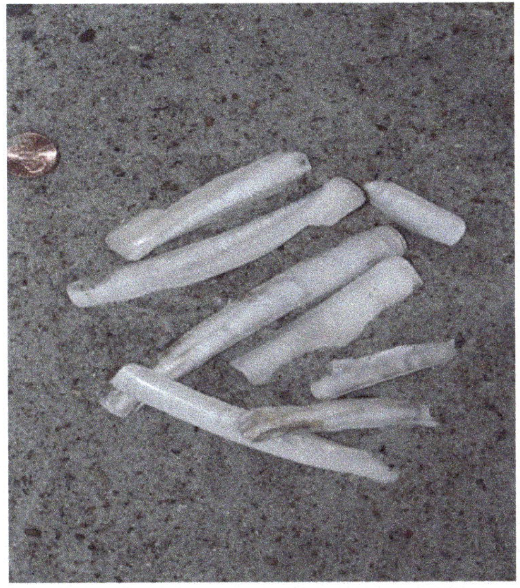

Identifying Features: Its shell is long and slender, slightly curved, and with blunt ends. The exterior is a grayish-white color. Habitat: In sandy intertidal area

This clam lives in permanent vertical burrows; it moves up and down by opening and closing the valves, which grip the sides of the burro

Jingles Shells

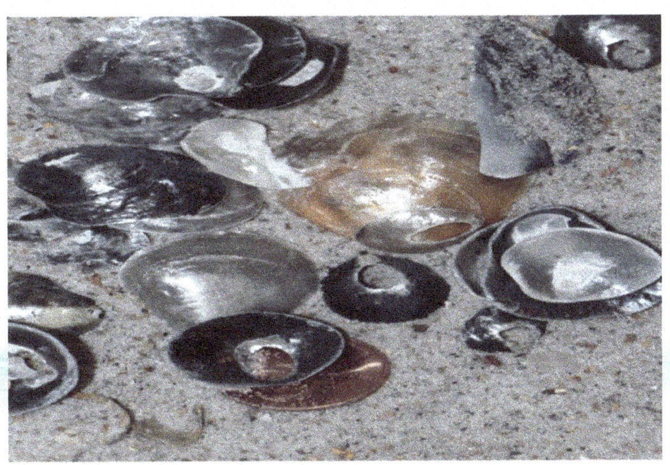

Identifying Features: They are translucent and very thin. Some have a hole. Their color includes white, yellow, and orange. The black ones have spent time in the anaerobic environment. They are very common in the Outer Banks. The right valve has a hole and is where the byssus passes through to attach the shell to a hard substrate. They are related to oysters: they lack the calcium carbonate thick layer present on the exterior part of the oysters.

Fossil Clams

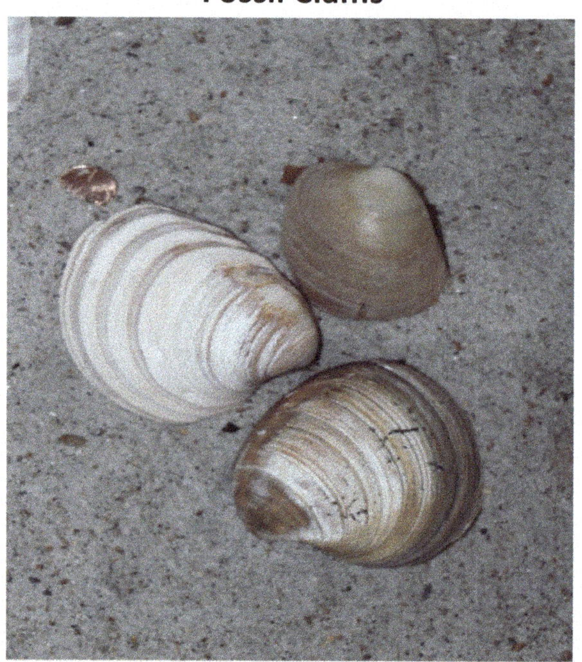

Fossil clams are larger and heavier than our modern clams. Fossil shells are very common in the Carolinas beaches. Some are 4 thousands years old, and others much older. The yellow/brown coloring is due to the oxidation of iron within the shell.

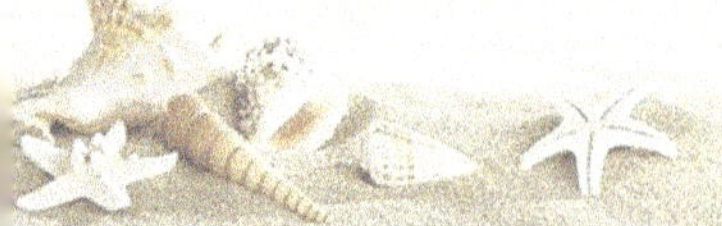

Scallops

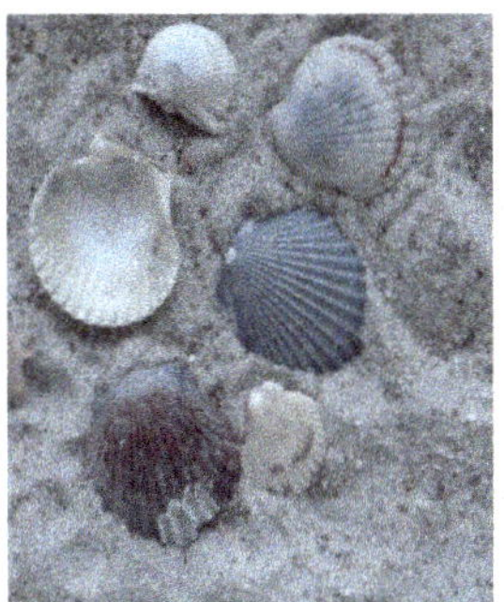

Identifying Features: They are round or oval. The right valve is generally more inflated than the left, and it has pronounced radial ribs. The shells become narrowed and pointed at the umbones, which has flattened, triangular extensions, "ears", on both sides. Most scallops can swim, clapping the valves, when escaping predators. They can be colorful, and the interior can have splotches of color

Tellins

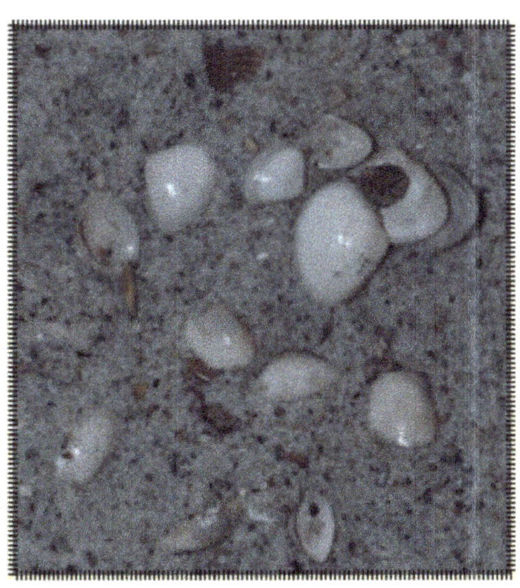

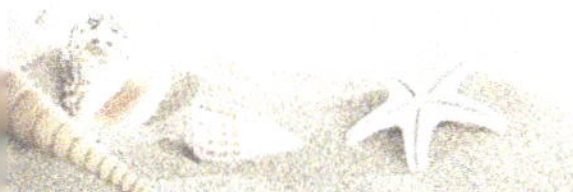

Identifying Features: Their shells are mostly ovate; the left valve is deeper and slightly larger than the right valve. The shell is either smooth or concentrically ridged. The hinge has 2 central teeth, with the front tooth being larger in size.

Tellins live in sand, mud, or gravel, buried horizontally on the left valve. They are mostly deposit feeders.

Coquina clams

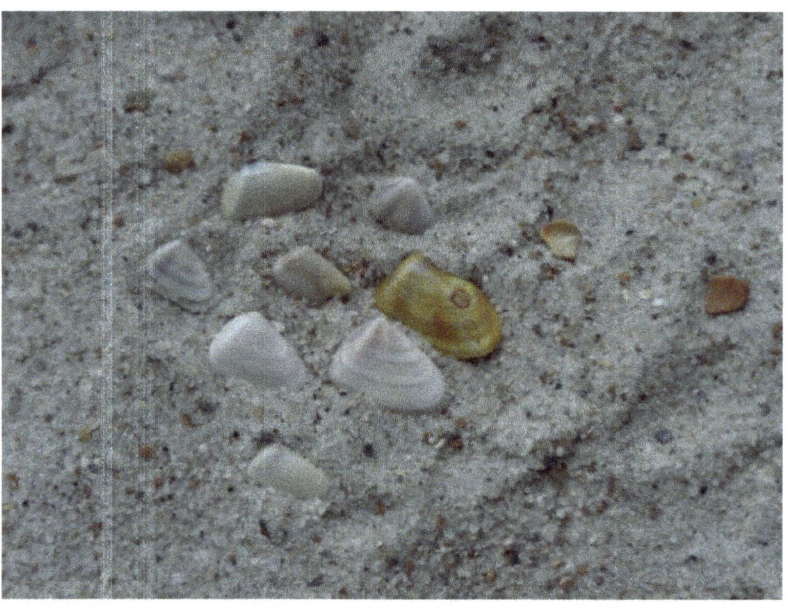

Identifying Features: They are glossy, wedge shape, inside margin strongly toothed, front end rounded. The exterior color could be whitish, or banded with pink, orange, purple, yellow, brown, or blue. They are the basis for the famous clam chowder. They live in the sand above and at low-tide line.

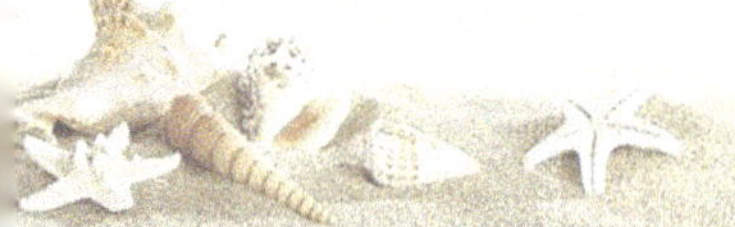

Angel Wings

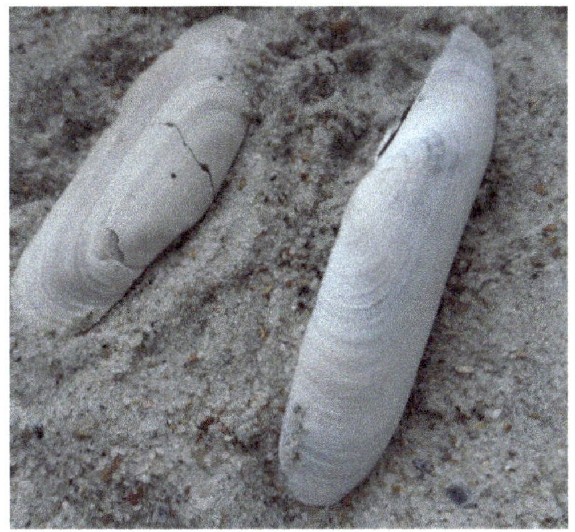

Identifying Features: It is fragile, whitish, wing like shape. The shells in this photo are old and bleached by the sun.

Pen shell

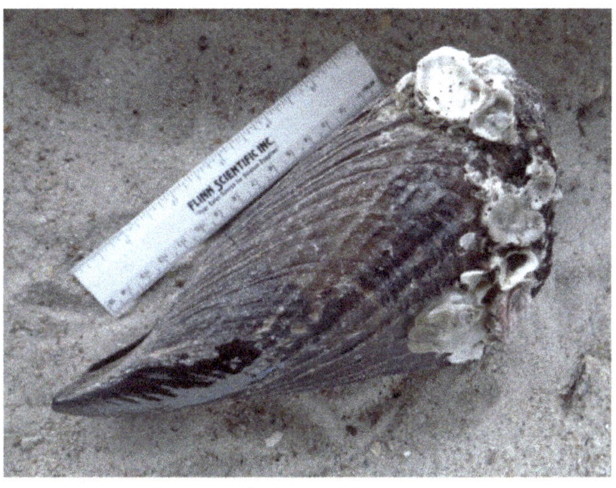

Identifying Features: It has a large, thin shell, fan shaped with radial ribs. The ribs may be spiny. It has a pearly layer interior, and a strong byssus. It lives in soft sand with the byssus attached to a buried stone or shell.

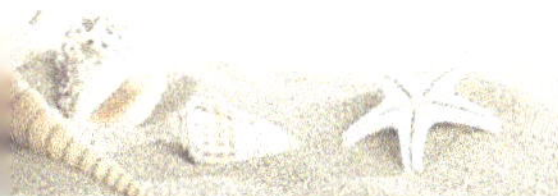

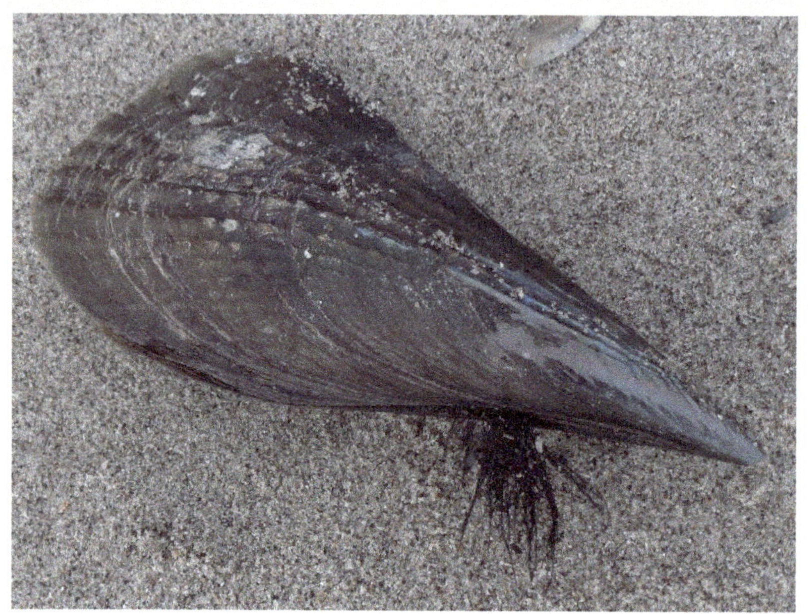

The byssus, made of strong protein fiber, attaches the shell to a solid substrate.

Pearly layer

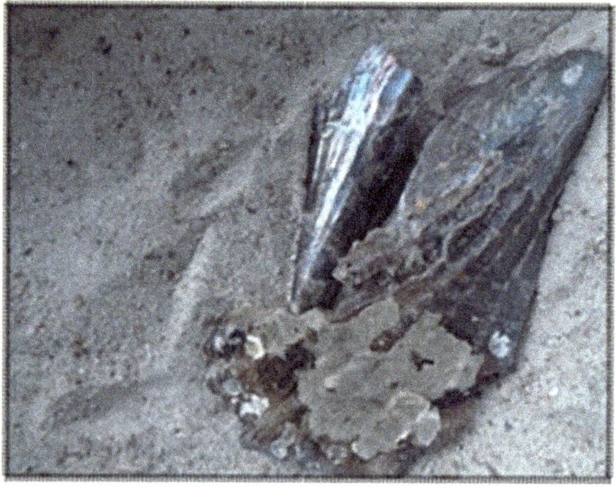

Just below the surface there is a pearly translucent layer. The light brown lacy spot is a colony of bryozoans.

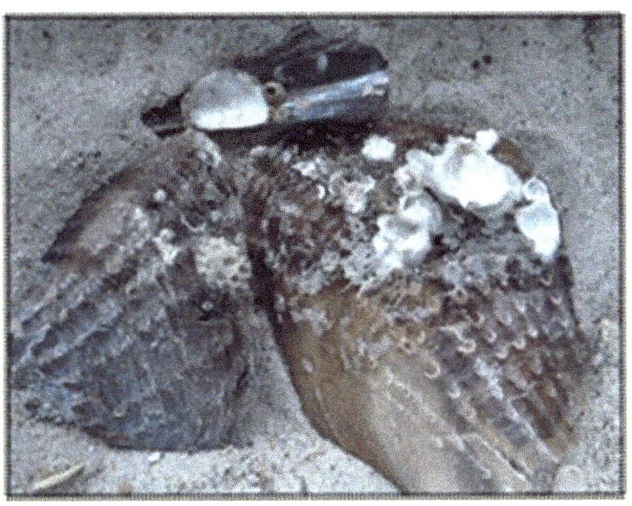

These old pen shells were home for corals, oyster, bryozoans, and barnacles.

Holes on shells

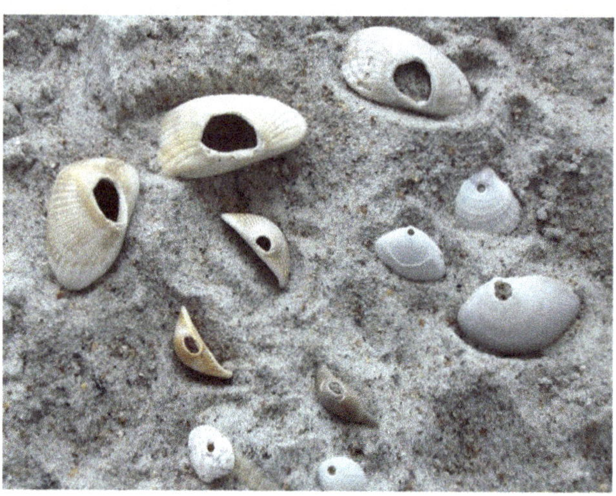

The Shark eye snail, also called the Atlantic moon snail, makes the holes in these shells. A shark eye drilled the holes in these shells when the animal inside was alive and sucked up alive. The process of drilling the hole can take an entire day if the shell of the prey is thick; approximately eight hours would be required to penetrate a shell 2mm thick. Penetration is done by the radula-a tooth studded tongue- with the help of the acidic secretion produced by a gland located on the proboscis. The gland squirts some acid, the radula rasps for one minute, and then the gland applies acid for 30 to 40 minutes, repeating the cycle until the hole is big enough for the proboscis to enter the prey. The soft tissues of the prey are torn by the radula and ingested. Often the hole is drilled near the umbo even though that area is the thickest part ofthe shell. This is because drilling close to the lower margin may represent a danger since the bivalve could snap the foot of the predator.

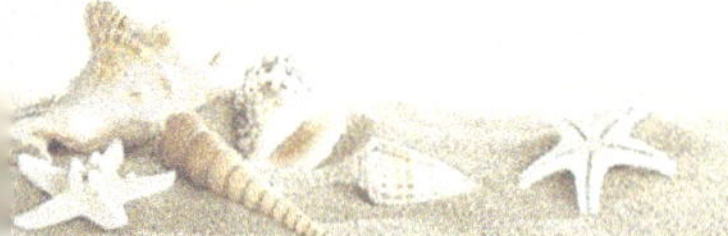

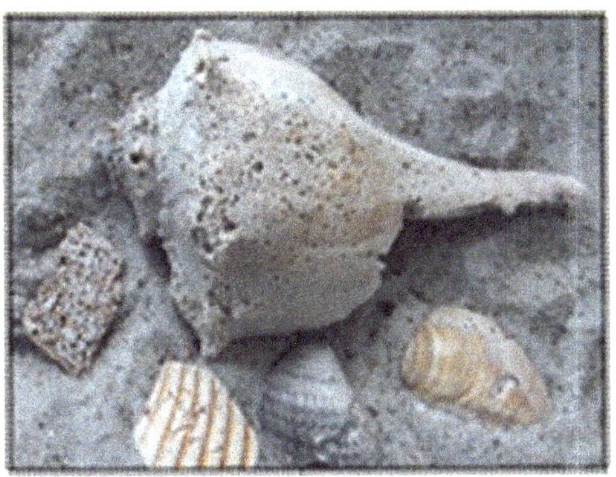

A sponge that found in the shell a safe place to raise its family made the little holes on this big knobbed whelk shell. The sponge settled on the shell-empty or with the animal still livingwhile in the water. After landing on the beach, the sponge died and what is left are holes on the outside and tunnels inside. The boring sponge is an important agent in the recycling of the calcium carbonate.

A boring bivalve, Gastrochena, looking for a home made the oblong borehole on the brown shell at the bottom right of the photo. Gastrochena is able to drill into a rock.

Broken shells

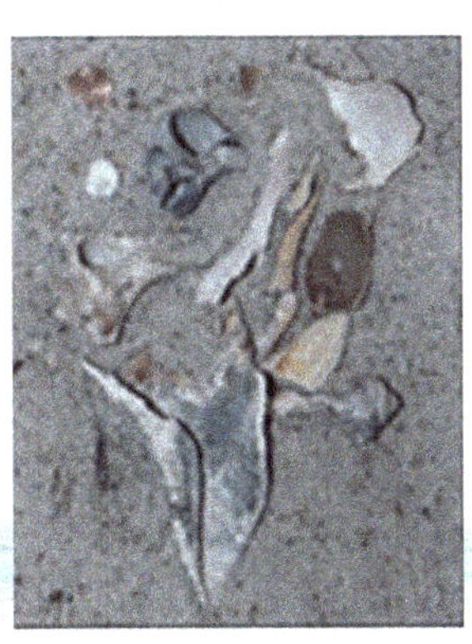

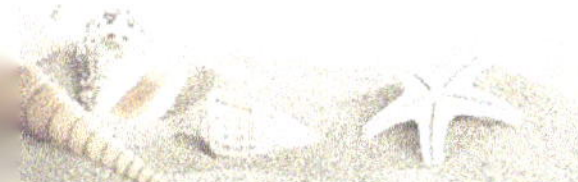

I like broken shells: they have a story. The top right shell piece is very shiny and smooth: the animal died recently. The dark brown piece shows the inside of the apex, the tip of the spire. The long white shell piece is a columella, the pillar around which the whorls revolve. The living animal was wrapped around the columella. The columella can be seen in the shells pieces located on the photo left side. The white lines on the large dark gray piece are little tubes, homes of some marine worms.

Grove marks on shells

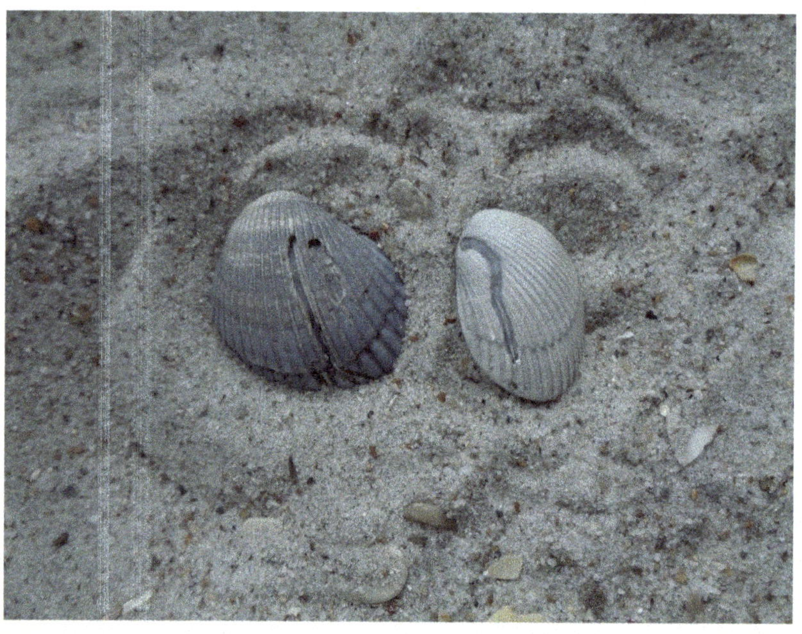

Bristle worms, using acidic secretion and the bristles present on each side oftheir body, made these grove marks. These marine worms used the shells-dead or alive-as a home, as a safe place to live. This is a very good example of commensalism, the type of symbiosis where one animal benefits (in this case the worm) and the other does not care.

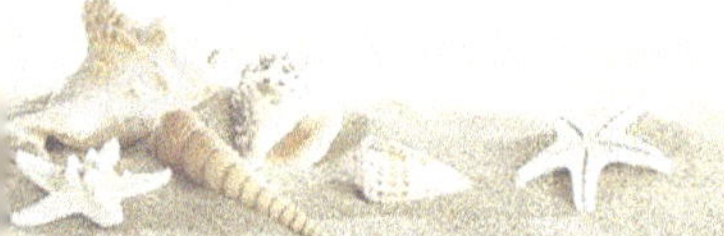

Settlers on a shell: sponge, tubeworms and oyster

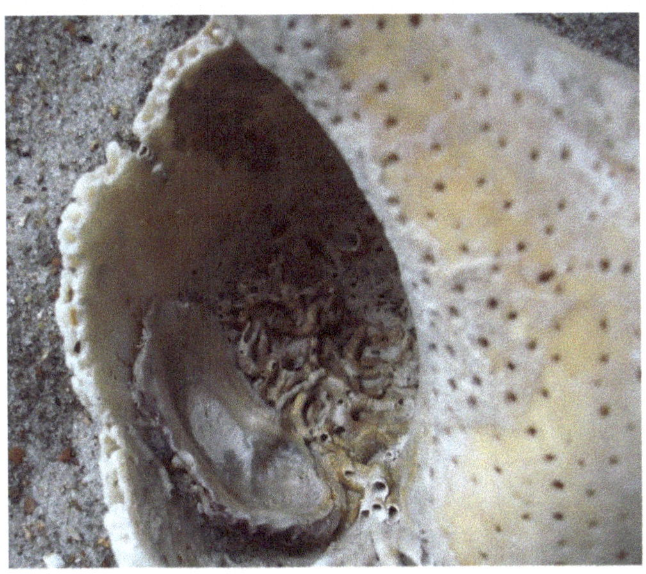

This piece of Whelk shell has a story to tell: after the animal that built the shell died and was still in the water, the larva of a boring sponge, an oyster, and of a tube worm settled on it. The larva of the sponge possesses special cells able to remove chips of calcium carbonate from the shell. After making a hole, the sponge makes tunnels that penetrate the whole shells. Tunnels communicate with the outside by little holes. The sponge's body projects from the holes small tentacles to collect food particles dissolved in the water.

The larva of a tubeworm found a safe place inside the empty shell and attached itself to it. For protection, it built around itself a wall of calcium carbonate, leaving the top open. From the top, tentacles were coming out to collect food particles. Since the location was good and the food abundant, the worm raised a large family.

The larva of an oyster, looking for a place to settle, found this old shell and glued itself to it.

Other Beach Findings

Red Alga

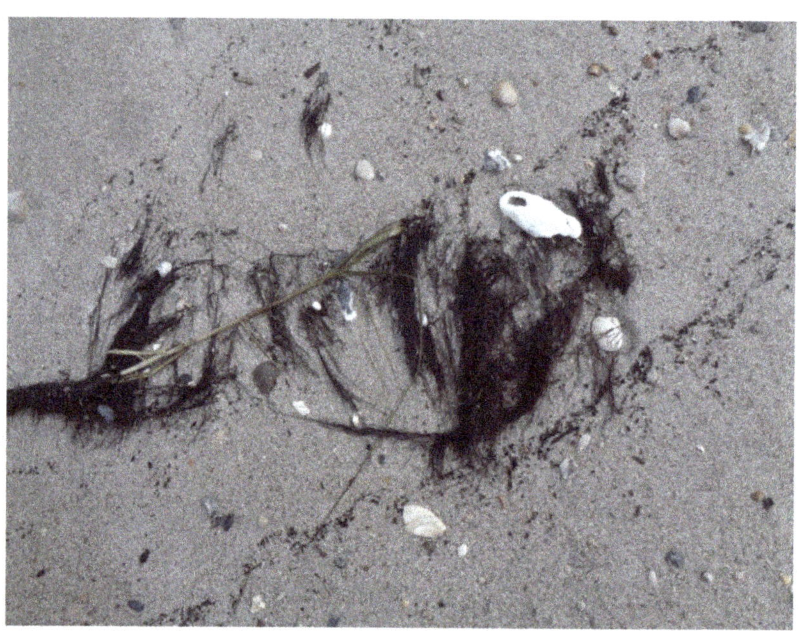

Red alga, also called red seaweed, is one of the plants adapted to live in the water. It is a plant, therefore it has chlorophyll, but it is not green. A red pigment masks the green color of the chlorophyll. The red pigment allows the seaweed to use the blue wavelength and therefore it is able to live few meters below the surface of the water. Light is a limiting factor for plants in the ocean because light does not penetrate deep into the water.

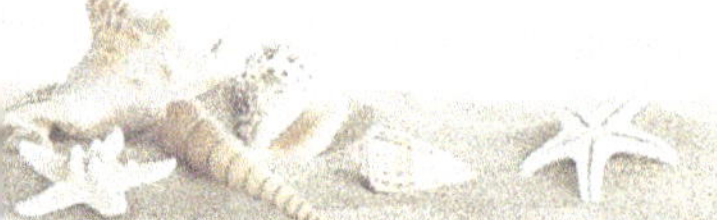

Sponge

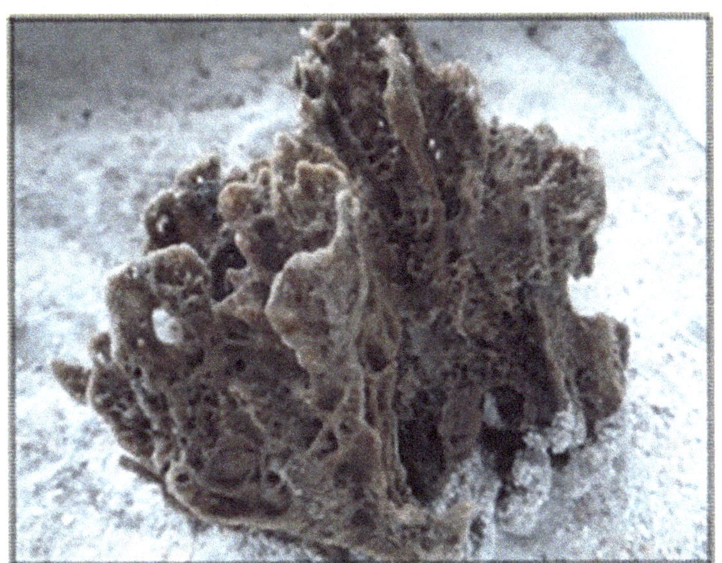

This is a sponge. It is an animal, not a plant, because it has holes; it needs to eat. Plants, since they make their own food using the process of photosynthesis, do not have holes; they do not need to eat. Sponges live attached to a substrate. They live pumping large volumes of water through their bodies and filtering out organic particles as food. The water enters the small holes and exits the large ones. Since they do not move, they developed ways to protect themselves from being eaten. Some of them just smell or taste bad, but other sponges produce toxic chemicals as deterrent. Pharmaceutical companies were able to isolate the toxic compounds, reproduce them in a lab, and use them in chemotherapy.

Sponges are an aggregation of specialized cells. If the cells are separated, can regroup and form a new sponge. Sponges do not have tissues or organs. Inside they have supporting structures called spicules. Spicules can be made of an elastic protein, or of calcium carbonate, or silica. This sponge was soft so the internal skeleton was made of protein, sponging.

Around the sponging were living or dying cells and therefore they could decay and smell bad. After taking the photo, I threw it away.

Skeleton of a vase sponge

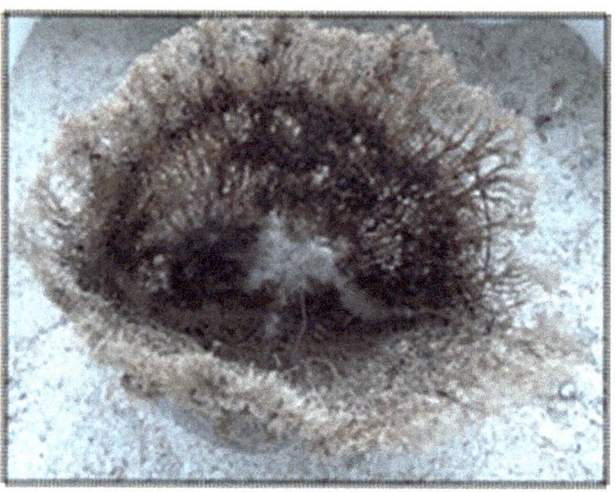

This is the internal skeleton of a sponge called "vase sponge" because of its shape. It is flexible, therefore is made of sponging. No body cells here, so I can keep it in my collection.

Sponge attached to a Gorgonian Coral

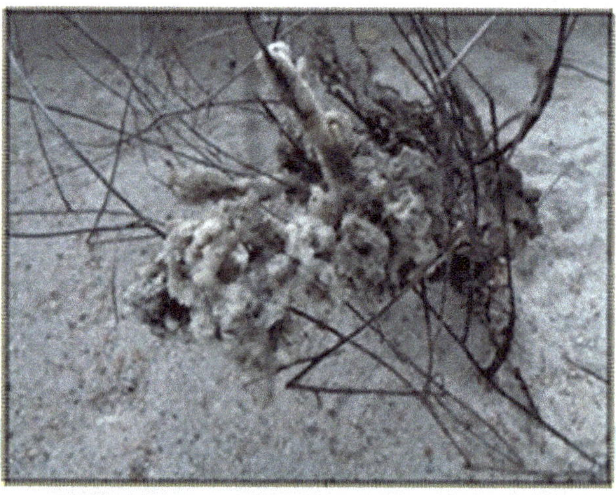

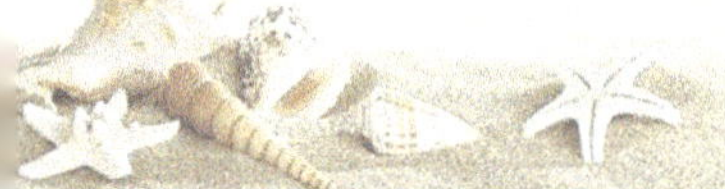

The white/grey masses around the thin branches of gorgonians belong to a sponge. It has big and small holes, very irregular shape, and it is soft. It is not just the skeleton and therefore I will not keep it.

Gorgonian Coral

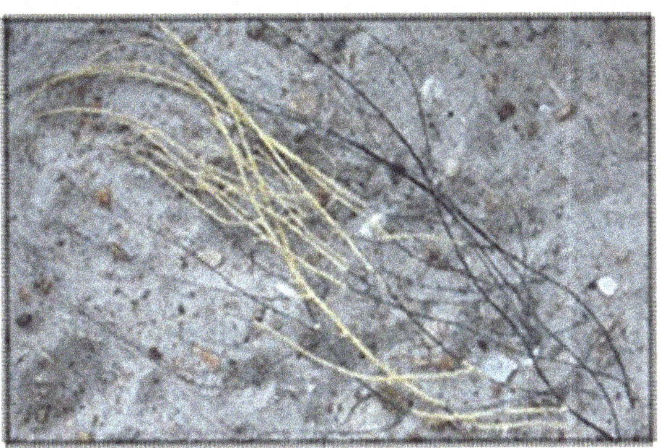

This is not a branch of wood; it is a gorgonian coral. Corals are very simple animals, the polyps. Each polyp has the shape of a bag with lots of tentacles on top. They live in colonies, and the polyps are connected to each other in such a way that food can be shared. This particular coral lives in deep water, attached to the bottom of the ocean. It is a filter feeder, getting the organic material dissolved in the water. What you see here is the dried up polyps (the yellow part), and its internal skeleton (the brown part). On the yellow part are many small holes, all the same size. They are the houses ofthe polyps. The corals that build the reefs live in shallow water, and have an external skeleton. Their main source offood comes from the symbiotic algae living inside the polyps.

Barnacle on gorgonian

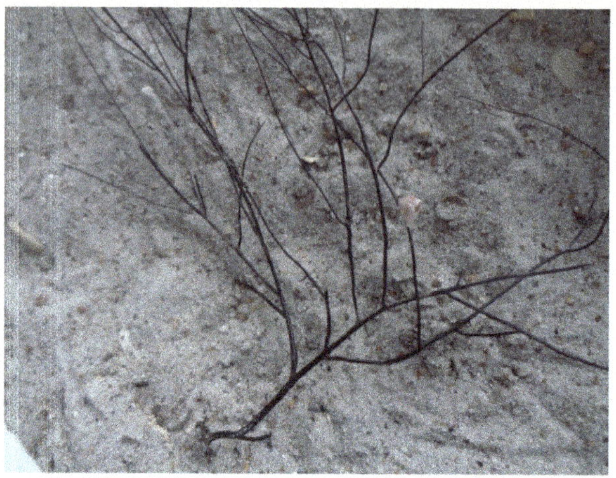

The black branch is gorgonian coral. The pinkish thing attached to the gorgonian is the empty shell of a barnacle. The living barnacle would stick out its feet from the large opening to collect food from the passing water.

The white coating around the tip of a little branch of gorgonian is an empty case of a colony of bryozoan. Below is the microscope photo of this case. Bryozoans are found attached to everything. When you see Ulace" you see a colony of bryozoans.

Bryozoan colony under the microscope X20

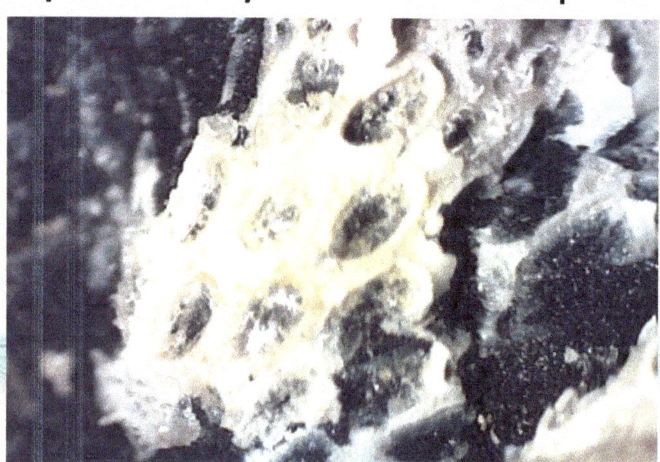

Each oval darker spot in the light area was the home of a little bryozoan.

Bryozoans built a colony around a little

branch of a gorgonian.

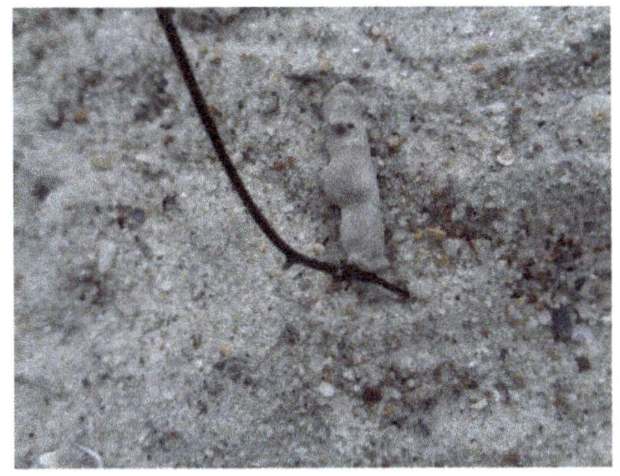

The lace" around the branch of gorgonian is a colony of bryozoans

Tubeworms on gorgonian

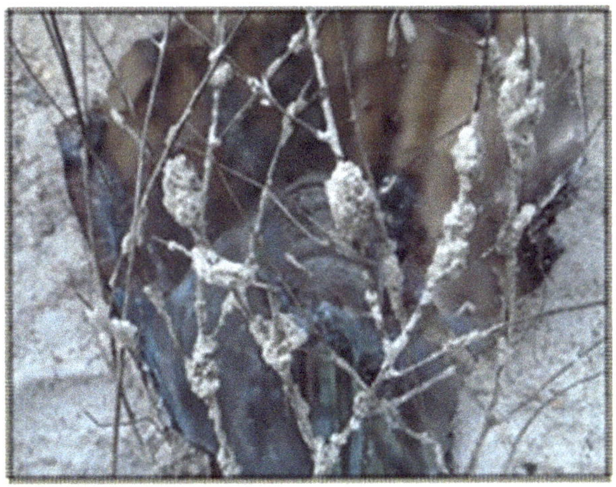

Tube worms colony around a branch of gorgonian coral skeleton. The tubes are made of sand and mucus. The holes are where the head of the worms came out to get food. On one branch of coral there is some "lace", some bryozoans.

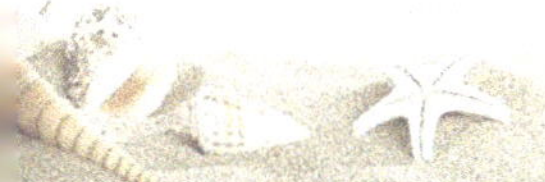

Hard coral on shells

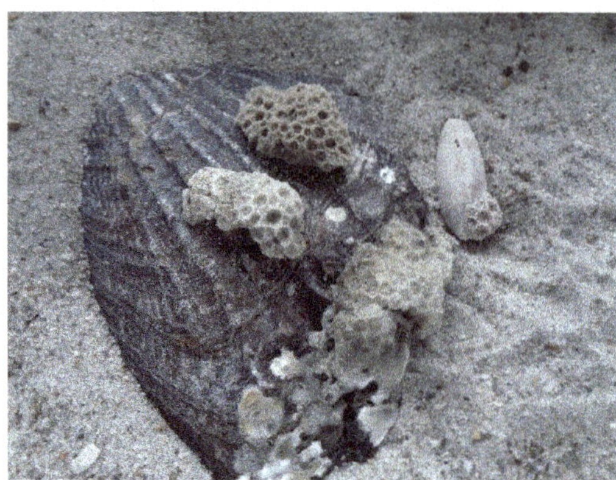

Attached to these shells are small colonies of hard coral, the coral that builds coral reefs. Each colony looks like a beehive; each cell was made by a polyp, the individual coral animal. The gorgonian polyps built their skeleton inside and of protein material. The hard coral polyps built their skeleton outside and of calcium carbonate. In this figure do you see colonies of bryozoans?

Drift Wood

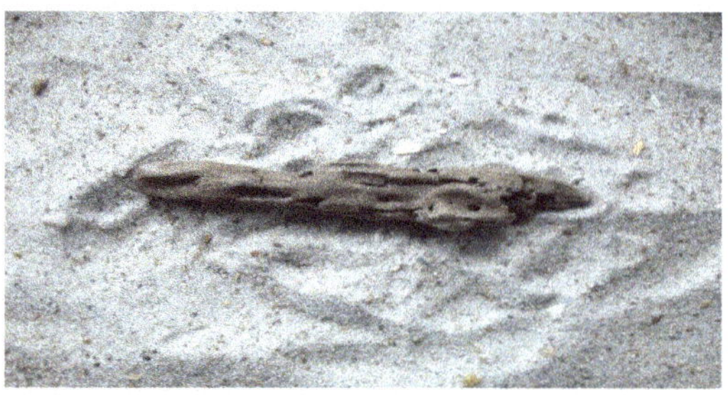

Shipworms made the tunnel in this piece of wood. Shipworms have the shape of a worm, but they are bivalves with a very small shell, which is equipped with razor-sharp ridges to rasp the wood. Wood particles are moved to the mouth and then to the stomach. In the stomach there are symbiotic bacteria producing enzymes to digest the wood. Shipworms do great damage to wooden ships. In Japan, people used to paint shark oil on the bottom of the boats in order to protect them from the shipworms.

Shell Pieces

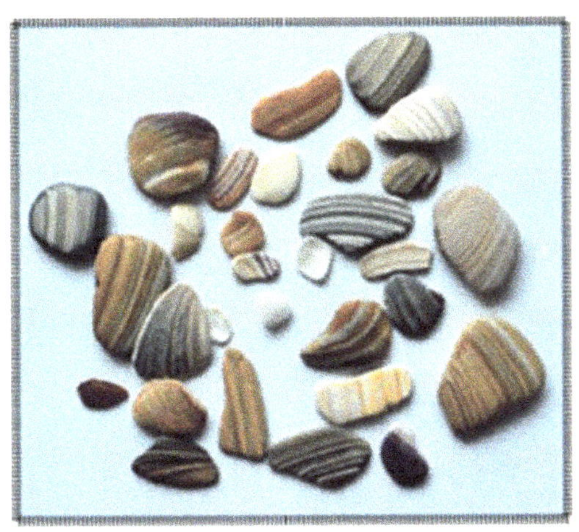

Because they are constantly being tossed and turned around by the waves, shells over time break into smaller and smaller pieces. Skates also contribute to the breaking process; they crush living shells in order to eat the animals inside. Birds break shells as well: birds hold the shell in their beaks, fly high and then drop the shell on a hard substrate. The shell breaks, the bird eats the animal inside and the pieces are there to stay. The pieces are polished by sand and water, and over a period of time develop smooth edges. Color and pattern present in the original shell are kept in the fragments. Eventually the pieces become grain of sand. The rate at which shells break depends on the energy ofthe beach. In high-energy beaches, where wave action is strong, the shells break faster, and they become rounded and smoother faster than the ones in low-energy beaches. Among patches of shell pieces, you can find whole shells, mostly small ones.

Mermaids' Purses and Organisms attached to them-

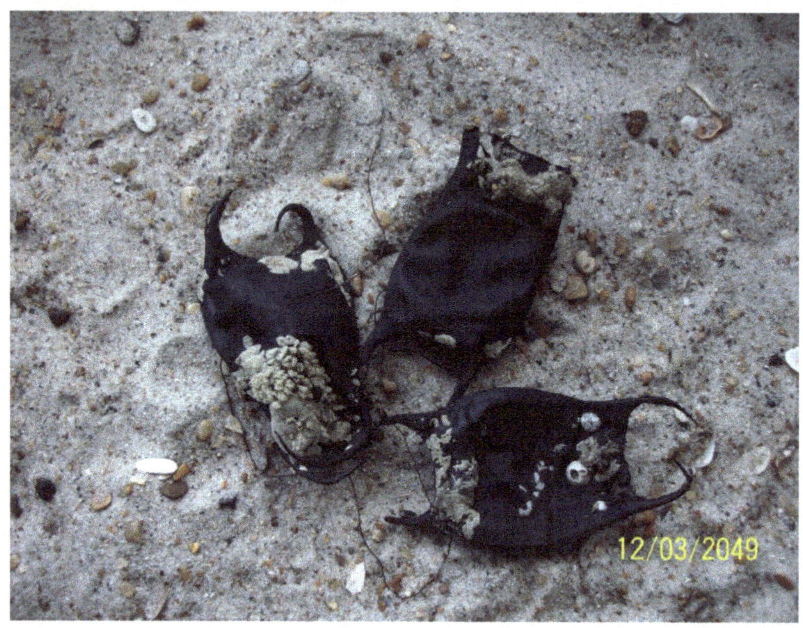

Skates lay their eggs in small pouches- commonly called mermaids' purses. The pouch is made of elastic protein, which is very soft while it contains the embryo. In the pouch the egg grows, over a period of 12 weeks, into a fully developed and independent little skate, ready to move on. After the baby skate leaves its home through a slit at one end of the pouch, the black case becomes hard like plastic and is colonized by several small creatures. A magnifying glass will reveal an interesting community. Little white volcanoes are barnacles, white delicate lace are bryozoans, mounds of sands are cases of worms, and little grains of rice are egg cases of gastropods. Below is the photo of the inside of the mound of sand.

Attached to the mermaid's purse

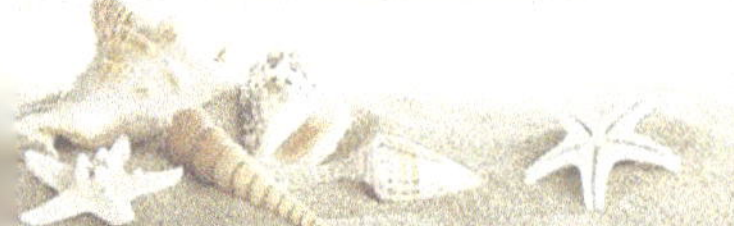

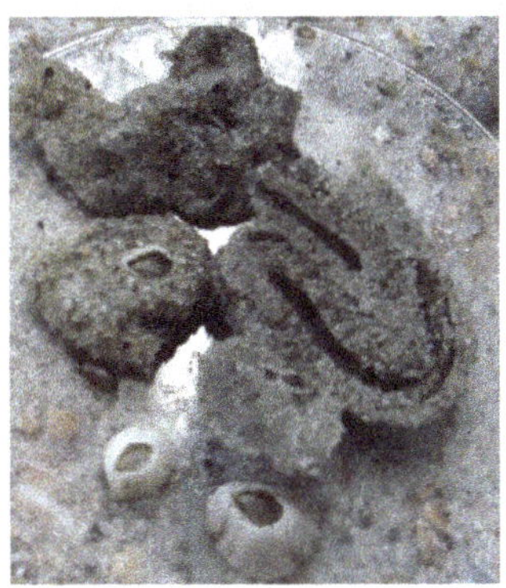

The mound of sand on the mermaid's purse is the home of a worm; the worm made it using sand and mucus. The dried up worm is in the grove. There are 3 barnacles around the worm. Two barnacles are very visible, while the third is hidden. The brown "seed" is a little mussel.

Shark teeth

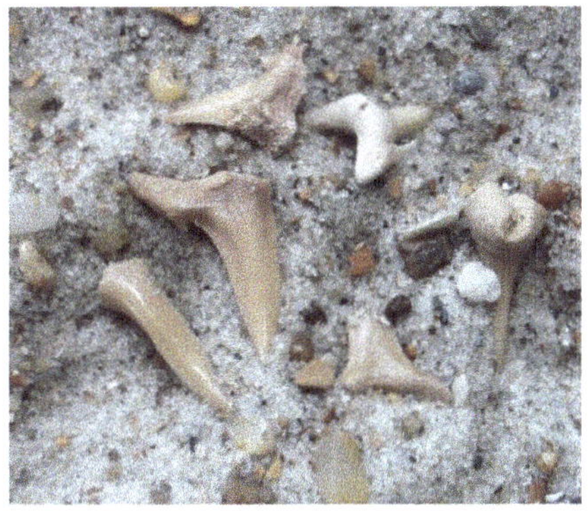

Shark teeth are shiny, light in color or black, usually less than 1/4 inch in length. The black ones are fossils and can be 5 million to 25 million years old. There are many shark teeth in the ocean because sharks, when the teeth are not sharp enough to tear up meat from the prey, get rid of them. A whole new crown of teeth that was laying flat against the gums comes up to replace the old crown. Sharks are known to be big eaters, always hungry. Not known is the fact that dolphins require much more food than sharks. Because dolphins are mammals they need to keep their bodies at a constant temperature for the enzymes in their cells to work well. Dolphins feel cold to the touch because they have a very thick layer of fat all around the body, but inside they are warm.

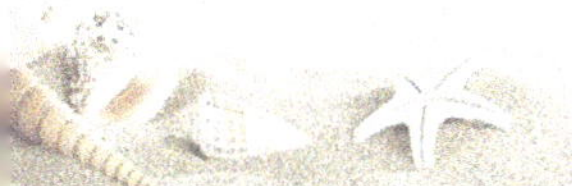

Bones of fishes and marine mammals

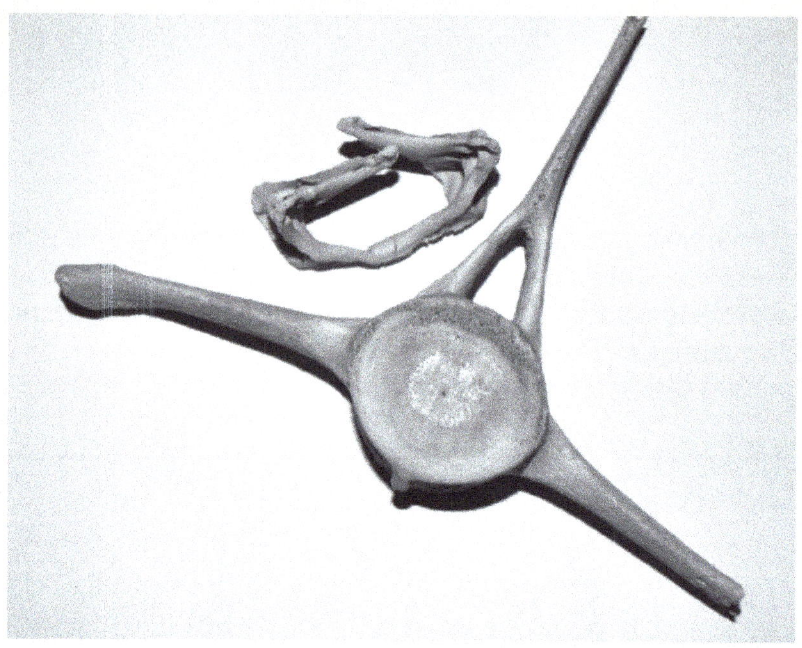

Whatever is in the ocean sooner or later comes to the beach. Fish die and the waves take them to the beach. Bodies of marine mammals sometimes end up on the beach. The large one is the vertebra of a mammal such as dolphin. When a dolphin or a whale is found dead on a beach, researchers from the local marine institute examine the carcass. After taking samples in order to determine possible causes of death, they dig a big hole in the sand and they bury the carcass. Eventually the carcass breaks down and the bones come to the surface. The round bone is the vertebra. The triangle hole above the vertebra used to contain the spinal cord, the large cable of nerves that connect the brain to every part ofthe body. Above the hole is a pointed bone where back muscles are attached. The small bone is probably the bone of a baby shark or of a skate since it was very flexible and very white. The skeletons of shark and skates are made mainly of cartilage, which is more flexible and lighter than bones. It's the same stuff your ears are made out of.

More Bryozoans

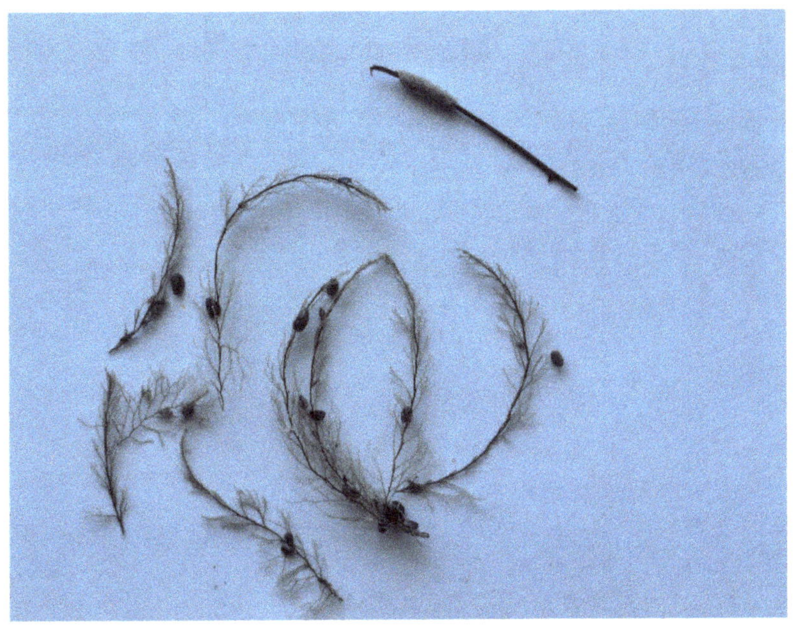

It looks like a collection of feathers. Each feather is a colony of bryozoans. The animals that built this colony are dead; this is their empty house. The phylum Bryozoa gets its name from looking like moss. Just like moss, bryozoans are very small and attached to hard surfaces such as rocks, shells, coral, and wood. The living animal surrounds itself by an encasement made of protein or calcium carbonate. Under a microscope each branch of the feather reveals a series of little cups attached to a thin "stick". A canal all along the stick is the way all ofthe little cups are connected to each other. When alive, the bryozoan lies on its back; when hungry it sticks out its feet through the hole, catching organic material dissolved in the water. When the animal dies it leaves behind its hard encasement. The black dots are little mussels that attached themselves to the bryozoan colony. The white lace coating the little stick is also a colony of bryozoans, the kind most commonly found attached to mermaid's purses, wood, and seaweed. The encasement of the feather bryozoans is made mainly of protein. The encasement of the lace bryozoans is made mainly of calcium carbonate.

Mended Shells

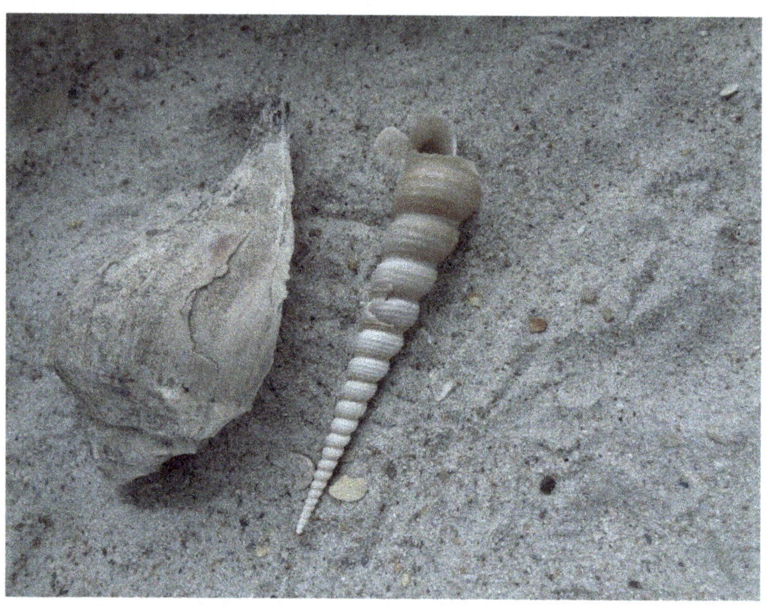

The mantle, the skin covering the entire animal is responsible for making the shell using the material brought in with the food. The living shell, when the animal inside is alive, is tossed around by waves and sometimes is pushed against a rock or another shell. If the shell is cracked and the animal is not hurt, it will be mended. The mantle repairs the crack by depositing bricks of calcium carbonate from the inside. The inside will be smooth; the outside will show the scar. The two shells in this photo show scars of a previous fracture. Shell collectors do not like mended shells because they are not perfect, but I think they are more interesting than the perfect ones; they tell us their life story.

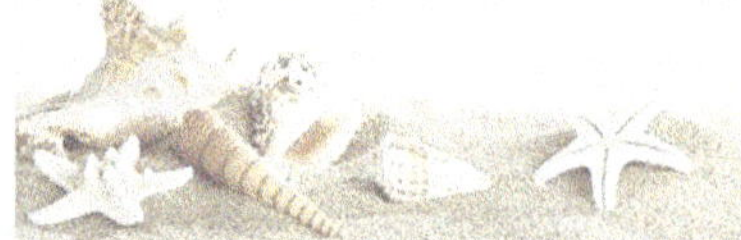

Sea urchin: dorsal view

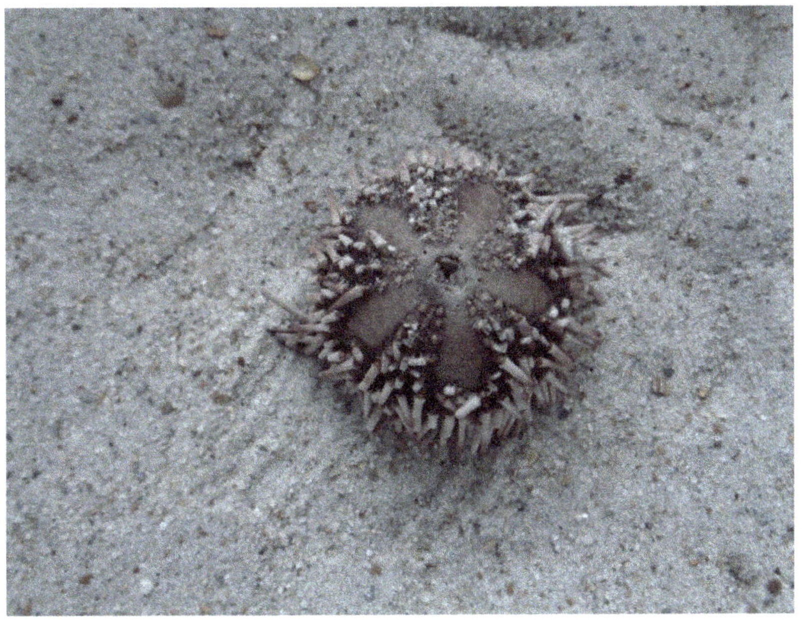

In the middle is the anus. Its skeleton is made of small plates of calcium carbonate fitting together; their total configuration is a star. The spines are mounted on ball-and-socket joints and provided with muscles so they can move in all directions.

Sea urchin: ventral view

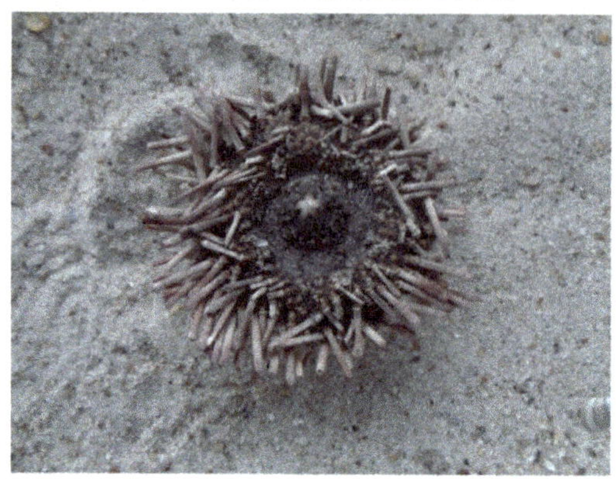

In the middle is the mouth, with five pointed teeth. Sea urchins feed mainly on algae and encrusting animals such as bryozoans. The scraping mechanism, made by the five teeth and a complex set of jaws, is called Aristotle's lantern.

Shells of Horseshoe Crabs

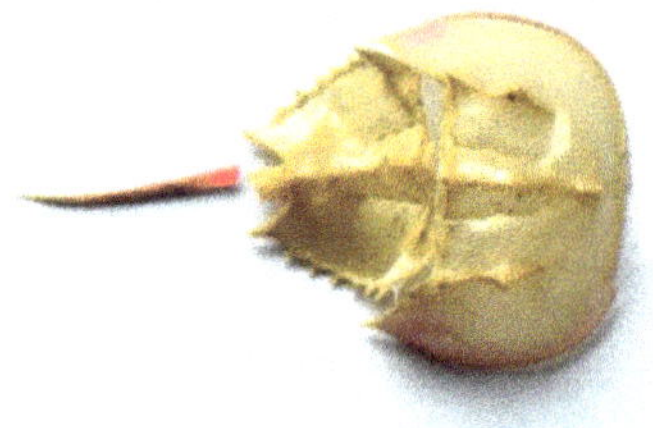

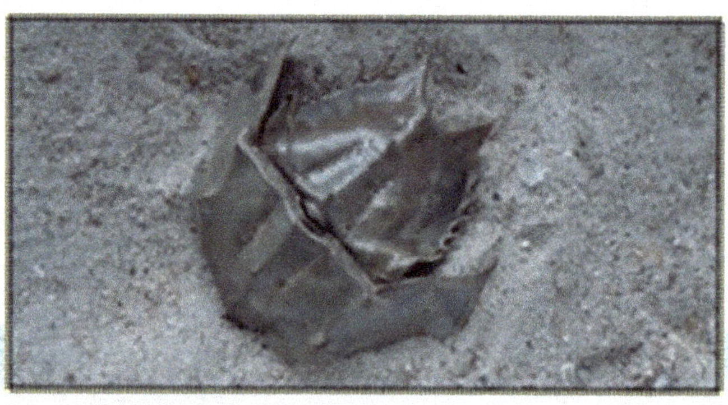

Horseshoe crabs are not true crabs; they are related to the longextinct trilobites and to today's spiders. Horseshoe crabs are encased in a hard skeleton and therefore, when they get bigger, they molt getting out of the old shell and making a bigger one. They have five pairs of walking legs, and a long tail used for pushing and for righting the body. They are often referred as "living fossils" because they have changed very little in the last 400 million years. They swim on their backs, but spend most of their time borrowing into the soft substrate looking for food: worms and mollusks. The male is smaller then the female. Their blood is blue, and contains chemicals able to detect presence of bacteria; these chemicals are used to check surgical instruments for bacteria in order to protect the patient from infection.

Activities connected to the beach

Collect shells or pieces of shells to make prints on T-shirts or on paper.

Make your own shell collection. Broken shells have their own beauty!

Decorate the frame of a mirror with small shells

If you have an electric drill, you can make buttons or pendants out of polished shell pieces. Place the piece on a cold wet towel and drill little at the time. Be careful though, if the shell piece becomes too hot, it will break.

Small and light shell pieces can be glued to around the collar of a T-Shirt, or to a canvas bag.

Polished oyster shells make interesting scoops or butter knives.

Write an haiku about a frozen instant at the beach

Dissect a bivalve, such as a mussel or a clam: identify the parts of the animal mentioned in the Quahog dissection

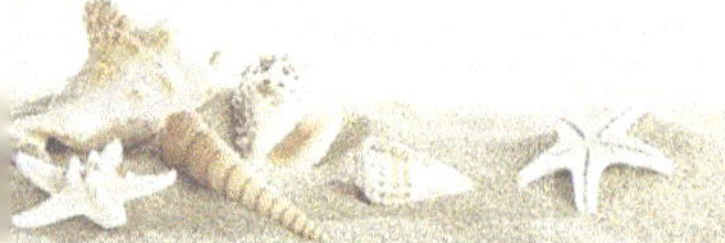

A simple shell collection

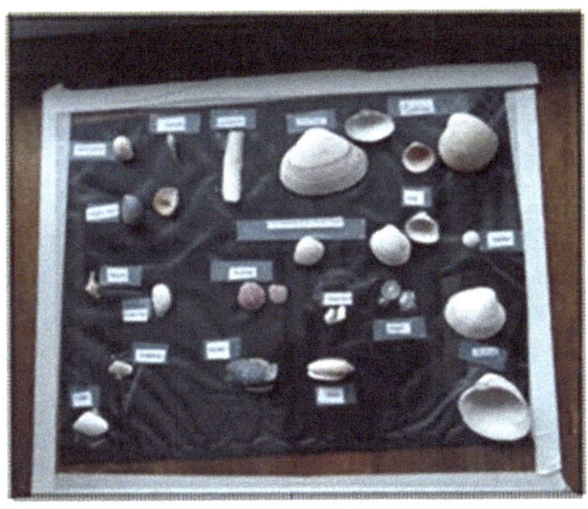

The shells are glued on a piece of glass

A Christmas tree at the beach

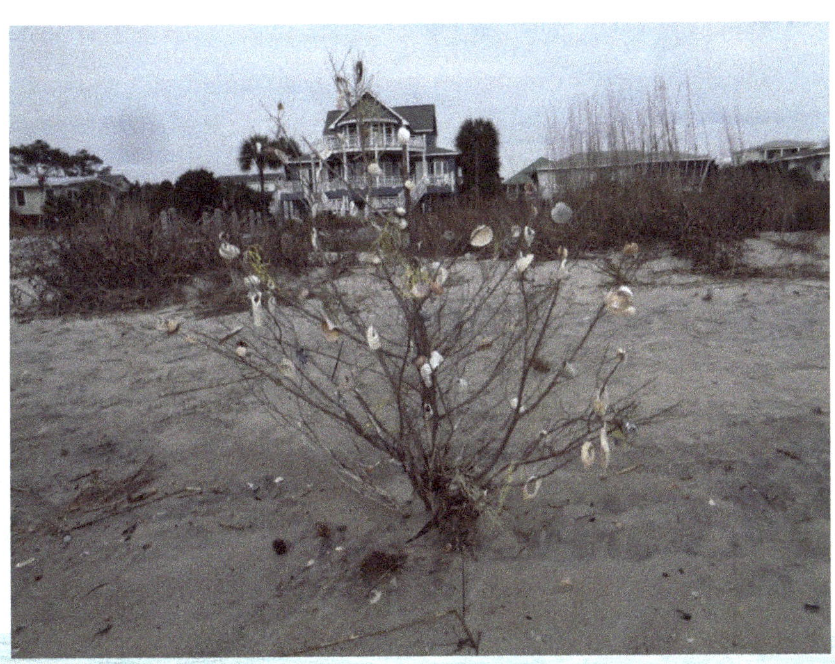

Glossary

Anaerobic: without oxygen

Apex: the tip of the spire in the gastropods shell

Aperture: the opening through which the foot of the gastropod animal comes out

Bivalve: a clam or oyster mollusk having two shells joined by a hinge

Byssus: thread produced by some bivalves to attach themselves to rocks or other stable objects

Cardinal teeth: in a bivalve, vertical teeth on the hinge

Carnivorous: feeding on the flesh of other animals

Central teeth: the teeth under the umbone in bivalve shells

Columella: the pillar around which the gastropod animal is coiled around

Detritus: small particle of plants and animal matter

Ears: in scallops the projections on the side of the umbone

Egg case: a structure enclosing eggs

Foot: the muscular structure used by gastropods to crawl and by bivalves to dig

Gastropod: single shell mollusk such as a snail

Gill: the organ for gas exchange: oxygen dissolved in the water enters and carbon dioxide exit

Herbivorous: feeding on plant material
Hinge: in a bivalve where the two valve are joined by the ligament
Larva: the young just out of the egg
Ligament: the protein elastic structure connecting the valves
Lip: in gastropod the edge of the aperture
Lunule: a heart-shape depression in front of the umbone
Mantle: the membrane enveloping the whole body of the mollusk, containing glands that secrete the shell
Muscle scar: in a bivalve shell the depression where a muscle was attached
Ocelli: primitive eyes that detect changes in light intensity
Operculum: the trap door in some gastropods that covers the aperture
Polyp: the coral single animal. It has the shape of a sea anemone and has a skeleton: outside in the reef building coral, inside in the gorgonians.
Proboscis: in gastropods a tubular extension of the head, with the mouth at the end
Radula: in the mouth cavity consisting of little teeth on a muscular ribbon; it is used by gastropods to eat and scrape
Rubble: accumulation of broken shells and stones
Scavenger: an animal that feeds on dead and decaying animals and plants
Symbiosis: two animals living together. It includes commensalism (one animal is happy, the other doesn't care), mutualism (both animals are happy), parasitism (one animal is happy, the other is not)
Umbo: the earliest part of the bivalve shell
Whorl: one full turn of a gastropod shell

Grazia Walker is a biologist. She was born and grew up in Varese, Italy. She has a Laurea degree in Biology and a Master

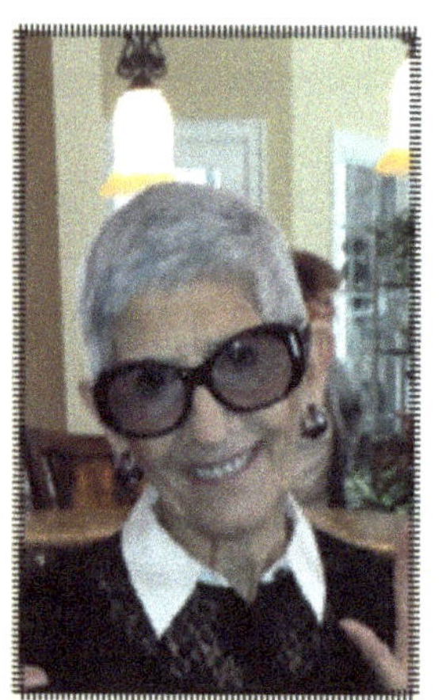

in Education. She taught Biology and Marine Biology at Kadena High School at Kadena Air Base, Okinawa, Japan. Grazia also taught 30 years for the University of Maryland in the US military bases around the world, mostly in tropical islands. When in Okinawa she fell in love with the ocean and the ocean is still her passion. Being an educator, she likes to share her knowledge on marine life.

Grazia lives in Charlotte North Carolina and her favorite pastime is walking the beaches of North and South Carolina.

www.beachwithgrazia.com

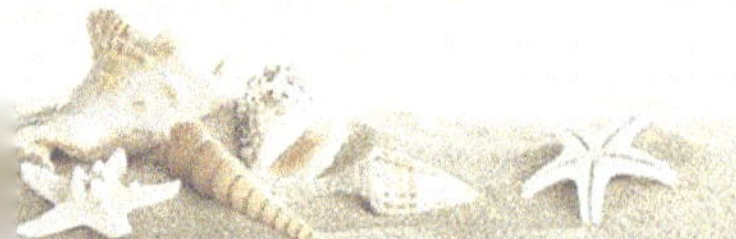

Shell Book Bibliography

Bachman, Karen: North Carolina Outer Banks, GPP, 2015

Barnes, Robert D: Invertebrate Zoology, Saunders College, 1980

Pearse, John and Vicki, Buchsbaum Mildred and Ralph:
Living Invertebrates, Boxwood Press, 1987

Pilkey, Orrin H- Monegan, Tracy- Neal, William: How to Read a North Carolina Beach, UNC Press, 2004

Shumway, Scott W: Atlantic Sea Shore, Falcon Guides, 2008

Witherington, Blair and Dawn: Sea Shells of Georgia and the Carolinas, Pinaple Press, 2011

www.ingramcontent.com/pod-product-compliance
Lightning Source LLC
Chambersburg PA
CBHW050014040726
47599CB00014B/1379